A SCAPE TO BERMUDA

Ian Macdonald-Smith

Presented to

_____

by

_____

<u>Acknowledgements</u>

Sincerest thanks to all my friends, too many to name, for allowing me to stay sane in the last five years - tolerating, encouraging, helping and a a result, allowing this book to happen. Special thanks must go to John Berg for helping me more than he will ever know; David Cox for being a great alarm clock, sounding-board and outspoken critic; Bruce Lorhan for educating me on many cultural aspects of the Island and Mike Wilson-Haffenden for opening the door.

Bill Zuill is a great friend - and a great writer - whose ability to understand and express emotion is immense. He has wisely tempered many of the environmental issues, about which I feel very strongly and without him the text would be sadly lacking.

My sister, Wendy, was responsible for the artwork on the map of Bermuda. Her talent speaks for itself, and I have had the benefit of that talent for this project and then some. My thanks also go to Julia van Beelen for providing the foundation of the map.

Two books have provided a wealth of information about Bermuda that is integral to this book - Willaim E.S. Zuill's 'Bermuda Journey' for many of the anecdotal stories, and Dr. Henry Wilkinson's 'The Adventurers of Bermuda' for much of the background on the early settlement of Bermuda. The Island is indebted to these men for their research and work - the books are well worth reading.

First edition published in 1991
Second edition 1995

Copyright ©1991 Ian Macdonald-Smith
            Hillcrest, 5 Clarendon Lane, Flatts, Bermuda

ISBN 976-8012-69-2
Printed and bound in Hong Kong

Limited editions available: 300 Leather bound books
                    33 Prints per image

At the mid hour of night, when stars are weeping, I fly
To the lone vale we love, when life shone warm in thine eye;
And I think that, if spirits can steal from the regions of the air
To revisit past scenes of delight, thou wilt come to me there,
And tell me our love is remembered even in the sky.

Thomas Moore 1779-1852

Foreword

It is indeed a great pleasure to have been asked to write the foreword tor this book. These magnificent photographs of our island depict the great love and concern for our environment that the photographer, Ian Macdonald-Smith, has for Bermuda.

"A Scape to Bermuda" shows the intense beauty of Bermuda and takes us on a nostalgic journey through the islands, stopping on the way to appreciate the environment and the need to respect and preserve it. Although the pictures are of today, Ian has cleverly depicted what could be yesteryear and while flicking through the pages, there is a sad realisation that some of these open spaces are in danger of development.

Locals and visitors alike will get the same enjoyment from looking at these superb photographs, interspersed with the island's history, its people and anecdotes, written by Ian and Bill Zuill.

On reaching the final pages, past land, sea and clouds, let's all hope that this will not be the only environmental record that we will have of this lovely island of ours but rather a keystone for its future.

Patsy Phillips
President
Bermuda National Trust

Introduction

Bermuda truly is a natural jewel; one of the world's most isolated islands and its northern most coral outcrop. Situated in the path of the Gulf Stream, the archipelago supports an amazing array of flora and fauna. Throughout the centuries many species have been introduced successfully to the islands. Bermuda's natural form 400 years ago was a blanket of cedar and palmetto forest with mangroves in the many protected bays. There was also an undisturbed abundance of fish and birds. The discovery of the American continent, the advent of the colonisation of North America and an unfortunate shipwreck brought Bermuda's virginal status to an end.

Our Island, totally insignificant on a global basis, meets at a critical junction. Bermuda's saturation point has been reached, and in many respects surpassed, consequently requiring extremely careful and philosophical control of our environment.

The management of such a small community has proved extraordinarily difficult and will be more so. Unfortunately it has been, and will continue to be, the environment that suffers. Only improved education will assure the Island's continued harmonious survival. Our present education system is barely adequate to prepare our most valuable resource for life in the unreal world. Reform is necessary but the system must not be changed merely for the sake of change. Rather we must analyse what our children need for their ability to improve our society. Much of Bermuda's society has been polarized politically, economically and socially. These problems must be addressed and rectified.

The pressures put upon our infrastructure are enormous, athough not entirely self-inflicted. Historically Bermuda has been independent and self-governing. However, change has been forced upon Bermuda by the role it has played as a geographic pawn of the power-mongering in the western hemisphere over the last four centuries. The Island has emerged from its past bearing the scars and the many memories. These can and must be put to good use.

As residents, we cannot deny that it is our luck and privilege to be here, meaning that the least we can do is preserve as many of our good traditions and as much of our environment as possible. Bermudians and visitors alike are responsible for the island's well being and cannot neglect that responsibility. Creation of a new environment is vital and must be treated much like a Japanese garden, planned, nurtured, loved and respected for the generations to come.

Bermuda has demonstrated that it can withstand most human abuse. However, modern Bermuda is only 50 years old and there are bound to be negative side effects on the community. The world has gained great technology and knowledge, to which Bermuda certainly has access and must use to its advantage, waiving short-term costs in favour of long-term benefits. The scapes within attempt to show that it is not too late to embark upon fundamental remedial measures to ensure the island's continued harmony with its environment. Bermuda is still a beautiful island but it would not have been fair or honest to allow this pictorial description to go unqualified. I love the Island too much.

Many of the opinions expressed in this book are strong, but they are intended to be constructive. Any deviation from the truth or fairness is completely unintentional and apologies are proffered now.

Ian Macdonald-Smith

LIGHTHOUSES   St. David's 1989

CASTLE ROADS   Castle Island 1987

OLD ST. DAVID'S   *Emily's Bay 1991*

I SAY CHARLES !   *Charles Island 1987*

BRIDGE HOUSE   *1989*

FOUND...   *St. George's 1991*

STRANDED   *Tucker's Town 1990*

WANTING   *St. George's 1991*

MAY 24   *St. George's 1989*

BERTHRIGHT   *St. George's 1990*

5

STRING ALONG

TUCKED IN   *Tucker's Town 1990*

SHORE IN WINDOW   *Tucker's Town 1989*

RAINBOWS   *Castle Harbour 1990*

NATURAL ARCHES

Tucker's Town 1990

RUNNING WILD   *Tucker's Town 1990*

SNAKES AND LADDERS   *Mullet Bay 1988*

MOTHER SUPERIOR   *Shelly Bay 1990*

NORTH FOLK PINE FOR   *Shelly Bay 1990*

MIDNIGHT BLUES   *Hungry Bay 1988*

CONCORDIA   *Camden Hill 1989*

POINTING FINGERS   *1988*

GRAPEVINE   *Grape Bay 1987*

GRAPE SHOT   *Grape Bay 1989*

ARTIFICIAL KID NEED   *Grape Bay 1986*

LIVE BAIT   *Grape Bay 1988*

GRAPE BAY THING   *Grape Bay 1986*

GRAPE BAY GRAPE   *Grape Bay 1987*

THE BURNING BUSH   *Devonshire Dock 1987*

DOCKSIDERS   *Devonshire Dock 1988*

THE MIDDLE EAST

BERMUDA GOLD   Devonshire Dock 1987

SILVER GREY   Lane Hill 1988

HAZY DAYS AND LAZY WAYS   *ENISLE EIGHT*

GOLD STANDARD
BOSTOCK HILL WEST 1988

34

TOWNSCAPE

City of Hamilton 1990

EITHER WAY   *City of Hamilton 1989*

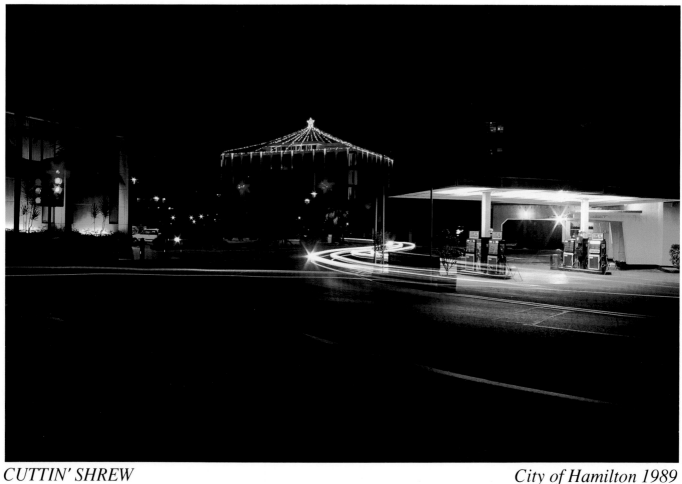

CUTTIN' SHREW   *City of Hamilton 1989*

THE GHOSTS OF DELIVERANCE   *City of Hamilton 1990*

LIGHTHEADED   *City of Hamilton 1989*

DEJA VIEW   Elliot Street 1988

WATERLOO HOUSE   Pitt's Bay Road 1987

YELLOW LINES   *Ferrars Lane 1987*

THE WESTERN FRONT   *Pembroke 1989*

TRI-CYCLISTS   *Astwood Cove 1988*

COVE PARK

Astwood Cove 1987

HALCYON DAYS   *Soncy Bay 1987*

43

CASUAL OBSERVATION   *Spectacle Island 1989*

DI-SOLUTION

Belmont 1988

RESURRECTION   *Belmont 1989*

FAIRY LIGHTS   *Harbour Road 1989*

PASS OVER   *Khyber Pass 1990*

SAFE PASSAGE   *Point Shares 1987*

LONG-SHOREMAN   *Warwick Long Bay 1989*

THE LONG WALK BACK   *Warwick Long Bay 1989*

LONGHAND   *1989*

CHRISTMAS DAY   *1990*

PUT OUT TO PASTURE   *Watch Hill 1990*

HORSEPOWER   *Horseshoe Bay 1990*

JEKYLL AND HYDE   *Horseshoe Bay 1990*

TWILIGHT ZONE   *1988*

DRY DOCK   *1991*   *STEP IN*   *1990*

SPAN YARD *1989*

CAN WE AFFORD IT ? *1990*

FLOCK OF SEAGULLS   1988

RACING FOR THE SPRING   1989

PSYCHIC TURBULENCE   1989

PHRU PHRU   1988

THE FLYER   1989

KNOT TODAY   *1989*

WHAT CAN YOU DO ?   *1988*

SPLENDID ISOLATION   *Gamma Island 1990*

MUSCLE IN   *Riddells Bay 1989*

WATERLOGGED

Jew's Bay 1990

CHILD'S PLAY   *Christian Bay 1988*

AMAZING GRACE   *Grace Island 1990*

GRACIOUS LIVING

Grace Island 1990

BREAK IN   *Dockyard 1989*

BREAK EVEN   *Dockyard 1989*

BAR KEEP

Commissioner's Point 1989

POT SHOT   *Jew's Bay 1989*

GREAT SOUND EFFECT   *Black Bay 1989*

WANTED:DEAD AND ALIVE   *St.James' Church 1988*

SPRINGFIELD   *Somerset Island 1988*

WHALE WATCHING   *West Whale Bay 1987*

BACK TO THE DRAWING-BOARD   *Somerset Bridge 1991*

ELYSIAN FIELDS *Ely's Harbour 1991*

HERON'S HAUNT *Wreck Hill 1987*

DEAD SET ON   *Palm Island 1990*

A FITTING START   *1989*

HAPPY SNAPPING

1990

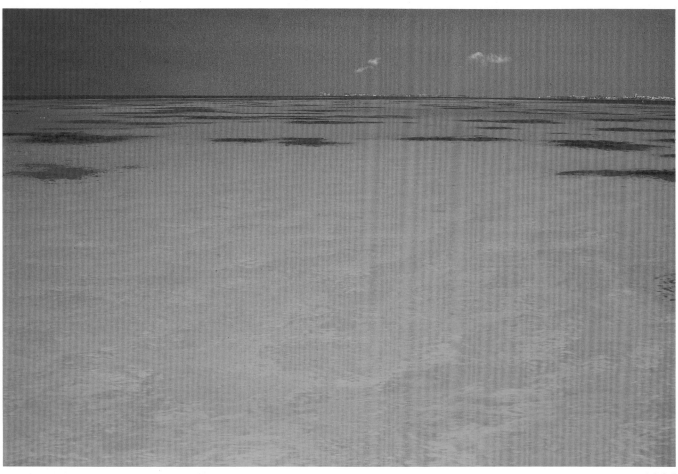

THE FAR EAST   *1988*

NORTH ROCK   *1988*

SINGLE-MINDED   *1988*

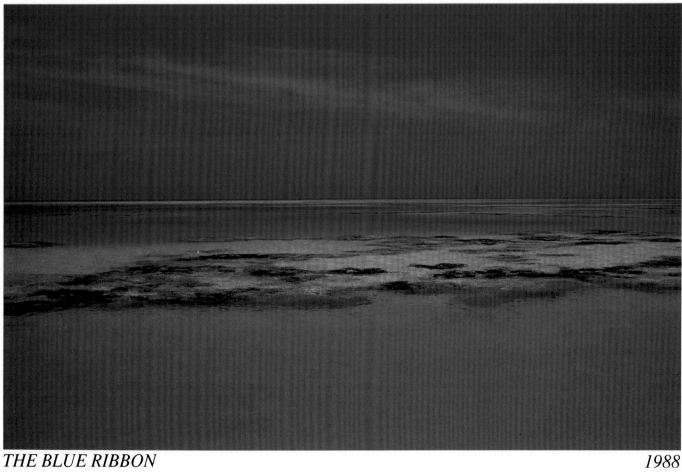

THE BLUE RIBBON   *1988*

SET IN MOTION   *1987*

CALM REFLECTION   *1987*

BREAKING AND ENTERING   *1987*

BRILLIANT DIMENSION   *1988*

UP THE SPOUT   *1988*

MOUND RUSHMORE 1986

GREEN AID 1986

HIGH EXPLOSIVE   *1989*

GABRIELLE'S PETTICOAT   *1989*

VILLAINOUS SALTPETRE 1988

UMBRELLA STAND 1989

THE ALTO PEACE   *1989*

FEATHER IN THE CAP   *1988*

TWO BIT CLOUD   *1988*

CUMULATIVE EFFECT   *1988*

MOUSETRAP   *1988*

SHEARWATER   *1990*

NUCLEAR RAIN   *1988*

WHISPERING PALMS   *1988*

KEEPING UP WITH   *1987*

TAKIN' LICKS   *1987*

AND SOME HAVE ONE OF GOLD   *1989*

LUNATIC FRINGES   *1986*

SNAKE CHARMER   *1988*

RAISE HELL 1986

LOOK WHO FRAMED CHARLIE AND THE PINK RABBIT 1989

DREAMSCAPE   *1987*

MEAN SEA LEVEL   *1988*

IN DUST REAL 1987

RAYS IN HEAVEN 1988

94

SPECTRACULAR

1987

A SCAPE   *1989*

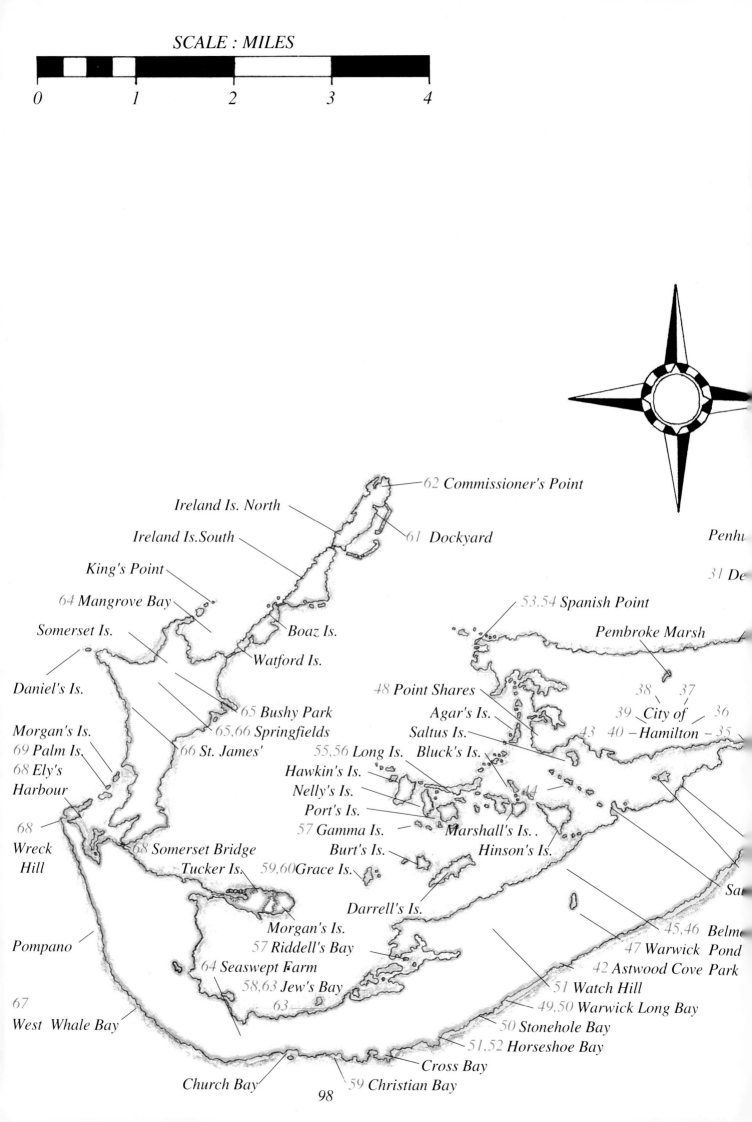

SCALE : MILES

0　　　1　　　2　　　3　　　4

62 Commissioner's Point

Ireland Is. North

Ireland Is.South

61 Dockyard

Penhu

King's Point

31 De

53,54 Spanish Point

64 Mangrove Bay

Somerset Is.

Boaz Is.

Pembroke Marsh

Watford Is.

48 Point Shares

38　　*37*

Daniel's Is.

39 City of　　*36*

Agar's Is.

65 Bushy Park

43　　*40 – Hamilton – 35*

Saltus Is.

65,66 Springfields

Morgan's Is.

66 St. James'

55,56 Long Is.　*Bluck's Is.*

69 Palm Is.

Hawkin's Is.

68 Ely's

Harbour

Nelly's Is.

44

Port's Is.

57 Gamma Is.

Marshall's Is. .

68

Burt's Is.

Hinson's Is.

Wreck

Hill

68 Somerset Bridge

Tucker Is.　*59,60 Grace Is.*

Darrell's Is.

Sa

Morgan's Is.

45,46　*Belme*

Pompano

57 Riddell's Bay

47 Warwick Pond

64 Seaswept Farm

42 Astwood Cove Park

58,63 Jew's Bay

51 Watch Hill

67

63

49,50 Warwick Long Bay

West Whale Bay

50 Stonehole Bay

51,52 Horseshoe Bay

Cross Bay

Church Bay

59 Christian Bay

98

Fort St. Catherine

St. George's Is.
5,6 Penno's Wharf
3,4,5 St. George's Harbour
11 Mullet Bay

Bridge House/State House

Paget Is.
Smith's Is.

14 Lover's Lake

2 Emily's Bay

14 Ferry Reach

17 Coney Is.

1 St. David's Light

Cooper's Is.

Bailey's Bay
13,16 Church Bay
15,16 Abbott's Cliff
Harrington
Sound

15 Wilkinson Avenue
17 Tom Moore's
8 Castle Harbour
13 Castle Harbour
Golf Course

Nonsuch Is.

Castle Is.
Charles Is.

Hall's Is.

4 Howard Bay
7 Caliban
8 Surf Bay

Trunk Is.
Rabbit Is.

23,24
Shelly Bay
Wistowe
Gibbet Is.

22 Flatts Village
18 Palmetto Bay

9 The Natural Arches
10 Mid-Ocean Beach

Trott Pond
Mangrove Lake

ark

ire

Devil's Hole
12 John Smith's Bay
12 Watch Hill Park
17,18 Spittal Pond
18 Pokiok Farm
19,20,21 The Pampas
21 Verdmont
23 Devonshire Bay
22 Brighton Hill
26 Camden Hill
25 Hungry Bay
26 Point Finger Road
32 Lane Hill
27,28,29,30 Grape Bay
3,34 Bostock Hill West
's Is.
le

otel

Sandys

Pembroke

St. George's

Hamilton

Smith's

Devonshire

Paget

Warwick

Southampton

Parishes

A SCAPE TO THE PAST, PRESENT AND FUTURE.

In 1603 when King James of Scotland succeeded Elizabeth I of England, the two thrones were finally united. Peace with Spain followed in 1604 and ended 18 years of naval warfare. The result of this peace was that the salt and tobacco trade which English merchants had in the West Indies was jeopardized. These merchants pulled their operations out of the West Indies and subsequently petitioned the King to allow the settlement of two colonies in America, where they had decided to re-invest.

In April 1606 James conceded to the petition, with specific orders that the "savages" were treated well and that there would be absolutely no plundering. The settlers were to be subject to English law and rights. On the 20th December 1606 Captain Christopher Newport led the expedition which arrived in what is now Jamestown, Virginia. The voyage took four months and arrived too late to plant crops. The ships returned to England to resupply the colony while the settlers attempted to survive.

Daniel Tucker, who would later govern Bermuda, built a boat and caught fish in the James River, which "did keep us from killing one another to eat". There were other problems facing the settlers that needed to be addressed for the colony's continued survival. Disease, Indian trouble and the ever present observation by the Spanish necessitated an absolute and strong governor whom the Spaniards feared.

This man was Sir Thomas Gates, who had served under Sir Francis Drake. Sir Thomas was given leave for a year from his post, commanding Dutch rebels against their overlords, the Spanish. On the 2nd June 1609 the Virginia fleet of nine ships and 600 emigrants set sail under the command of veteran seaman Admiral Sir George Somers, who had been a privateer in the West Indies at the same time as Sir Walter Raleigh.

Sir George and Sir Thomas both decided to sail in the Sea Venture after a disagreement over precedence. For almost two months the fleet sailed towards Jamestown until a huge storm hit on the 24th July which lasted for three days and separated the fleet. The Sea Venture started to sink, taking in water for three days as the crew, passengers and even Sir George and Sir Thomas desperately bailed the ship. When all hope and energy had failed, Sir George sighted land, renewing everyone's vigour until the ship lodged between two reefs.

The ship's dinghies were launched, taking the 150 people and all of the remaining supplies to shore. There was also time to strip the Sea Venture of all her tackle, iron and a few beams. The party discovered that they had happened upon "the dreaded islands of Bermuda....called commonly the Devils Islands, which are feared and avoided of all sea travellers alive, above any other place in the world..." This was written by William Strachey, who was going to Virginia as the secretary-elect. His account of the shipwreck was reputed to have been read by William Shakespeare, thus inspiring "The Tempest".

On the first day of the shipwreck, Sir George caught enough fish to feed the entire contingent. The Devils Islands provided enough lumber, materials and food for the shipwreck party's continuance. Two ships were built to transport the emigrants to Jamestown; the Deliverance, built by Sir Thomas using the remains from the Sea Venture and the Patience, built watertight by Sir George entirely of Bermuda cedar after another disagreement forced the two men to build separate barks. On 10th May 1610 the two ships sailed away and in a fortnight were in Jamestown to the relief of the sixty remaining settlers.

Sir George Somers returned to Bermuda to gather needed food for the colony but died shortly after arriving. His nephew, Matthew, captain of the Patience, buried Sir George's heart in Bermuda and carried his body to England with the approval of most of the crew. News of the island was reported, and in 1612 a ship, the Plough, arrived with Governor Richard Moore and Bermuda's first sixty settlers.

Bermuda turned out to be disappointing for the Adventurers who invested 2,000 pounds and expected a much greater return than the island provided. King James ordered the islands to be divided into eight tribes, named for each of the principal Adventurers, then subdivided into 400 shares of 25 acres, sold for 13 pounds each. St. George's, the "general land" was the capital and undivided. Since the initial settlement, Bermuda has struggled to survive economically, socially and, more importantly, environmentally. The following articles try to show not only how unique this archipelago is with its fascinating history and its potential for a great future.

Only if we could travel back in time to see Bermuda as it was, before man interfered with nature, could we appreciate how much we have inadvertantly destroyed. It is not too late to restore Bermuda to a semblance of her former glory as an enchanting paradise with co-ordinated effort by the whole community.

LIGHTHOUSES
Mount Hill, St.David's

The much needed lighthouse was completed in 1879 on Mount Hill after three years work. On the left is 61-acre Smith's Island, named for Sir Thomas Smith, the first governor of the Somers Island Company.

St. David's is Bermuda's easternmost island and was originally 510 acres. The name originated in 1612 when the first colonists countered the patron saint of England (St George) with that of the patron saint of Wales. Carter House in St. David's is the oldest dwelling on the island. Christopher Carter was one of those shipwrecked and he remained behind with Edward Waters when the Patience and the Deliverance set sail for Jamestown.

Carter had been involved in two mutinous incidents and fearing retribution from Sir Thomas, did not want to continue to Virginia. Waters was one of Sir George's servants who killed another sailor. Waters was tied to a tree with the dead sailor but was rescued. When the ships set sail, he was left behind.

Later Carter was one of the "Six Governors" who ran the island after the departure of Governor Moore who returned to London to answer criticism from the settlers and the Adventurers. The control was varied; one Governor was very strict, another went pirating. Carter was especially lax and in his month "Not a hoe, axe, pickaxe or shovel was so much as once heard in the streets, nor an oar seen or heard unless when their stout stomachs compelled them to it".

St. David's Islanders were isolated and ignored for centuries with no roads until the 1890s despite petitions for improvements 60 years earlier. The two islands were finally joined in 1934 by the Severn Bridge although the St. David's Islanders were apprehensive of this violation of their carefully nurtured insularity. There was a "them"and "us" syndrome between the mainlanders and islanders, often called "Mohawks". This slur - now a proudly carried nickname - referred to the large percentage of Native American ancestry on the island.

In 1941 St. David's was transformed. The "Bases for Destroyers" deal made between Britain and the United States during the Second World War forced the Bermuda government to buy land and lease it to the US for 99 years. Those "facilities" were 259 acres of old St. David's hills which were unceremoniously levelled and pushed into the sea. The landfill buried and connected other islands to give a total area of 680 acres for the base in St. David's. "It was rumoured that President Roosevelt had declared that he wanted the base to look Bermudian and thus be something of which both Americans and Bermudians might be proud," according to W.E.S. Zuill's Bermuda Journey.

On the base's 50th Anniversary, the US might find it in its heart to honour the sacrifice of the St. David's Islanders and fulfil Roosevelt's wish. The base is a blot on the landscape, with tacky buildings, treeless roads and a hideous chainlink avenue that St. David's Islanders must drive through to get to the rest of the Island. The US must respect that Bermuda wants and cherishes, architecturally, aesthetically and environmentally sound areas. Despite the benefits that the American presence has brought, our tenants are most negligent in the tending of their "garden".

OLD ST. DAVID'S
Emily's Bay Lane, St. David's

Although the majority of the islanders were seamen, St. David's also had a strong agricultural tradition. The island was one of the first areas to be cultivated for tobacco and until the base intruded, much of the island was farmland. Through the centuries the islanders turned their hands to many crops - arrowroot, potatoes, onions and Easter Lilies - which in turn failed due to pests, disease, foreign tariffs and competition. The history of Bermuda's agriculture will unfold as we journey through the island.

Emily's Bay has no definite name origin but other bays on the island have feminine names (Annie's, Dolly's, Grace's, Ruth's) demonstrating the islanders traditional respect for women.

CASTLE ROADS
Castle Island, St. George's

Castle Island is a three and a half acre island at the gateway to one of Bermuda's earliest harbours. "Governor Moore,who brought the first deliberate settlers in 1612, managed to build eight or nine simply designed wooden forts to protect the entrances into St. George's and Castle harbours against the Spaniards and in defence of the little town. The very fact that the uncharted reefs and channels made the island hard to approach in safety also made them easy to defend. The ring of earliest forts included King's Castle on Castle Island which commanded the only channel into Castle Harbour - Castle Roads - and was Moore's first and best fort... In 1614 two Spanish ships attempted a feeble attack on the island. When the small garrison of a dozen men on Castle Island saw the two ships heading in, they had only a few shots left for their guns. In the ensuing excitement, their one barrel of gunpowder got knocked over and spilled. Governor Moore, an excellent gunner, himself fired the two shots that were left, and the Spanish ships turned tail and sailed away, perhaps surprised that there were manned forts in the islands they had only lately heard were occupied by the English. From then on the fortifications on such a vital spot as Castle Island were continuously added to, made more permanent, extended".(Terry Tucker- The Islands of Bermuda)

Later, Castle Island was joined to Tucker's Town by a causeway, which has since disappeared, and the island was used as a hospital. Its isolation from the mainland meant it was a safe haven from yellow fever and other diseases which ravaged the rest of Bermuda.

The island is now in the care of the Department of Agriculture and Fisheries and permission should be obtained before a visit. The delicate buildings and grounds must be protected for future generations.

I SAY CHARLES!
Charles Island, St. George's

Charles Island, immediately south of Castle Island, derives its name from Prince Charles - the future Charles I. Governor Moore fortified the 3.5 acre island with the first stone building in Bermuda to command the entrance to Castle Harbour. Sadly, this structure has disappeared.

This panorama was taken in April when the water is still very clear, due primarily to low plankton counts and minimal boat traffic. The island has no human use but it is an important bird sanctuary for the nesting of longtails and cahows - the utmost care must be taken to protect these nesting sites. Bermuda's only endemic bird, the Cahow, was thought to be extinct until a couple of pairs were discovered in the 1950s. There are now an estimated 45 nesting pairs, but they remain an endangered species. When the first settlers arrived, there were thousands of Cahows which presented an abundant supply of food which was easy to harvest. Needless to say, Cahows soon became very scarce.

BRIDGE HOUSE
Bridge House, St. George's

Bridge House, on Kent Street, is a Bermuda National Trust owned property which is named for the bridge which once crossed a creek at this point. In the early 1700s, it was leased to several Governors as their official residence and an old plan shows that one corner of the property contained a special storage tank for the Governor's whale oil. The Governor had the right to oil from each whale captured, and had to have a place to store what was then a valuable commodity.

Whaling was an important industry for Bermuda from the 1600's until the early years of this century. Whaling was particularly important to St. David's Islanders and when a whale's spout was sighted off the South Shore, boats would be manned and would set off in pursuit. When a boat was close enough, the whale would be harpooned and after a lengthy fight, the whalers would attack it with lances and pull it to shore where the blubber would be cut off and cooked in iron pots until it turned to oil. The meat was eaten and the bones used for a variety of purposes.

FOUND. . .WANTING
Town of St. George's, St. George's

The 700 acre island and the town are named after St. George, patron saint of England, and Sir George Somers. St. George's was the capital of the colony, until it moved to Hamilton on January 1st, 1815. The decision was not welcomed by St. Georgians but was necessitated by practicality - the opening of the Great Sound to Vessels drawing 9 feet and the naval dockyard being built on Ireland Island, Sandys.

The sailing ship (left, foreground) is a replica of the Deliverance and was constructed by the Bermuda Junior Service League in the early 1970s. The original was built at Buildings Bay.

The oldest building in Bermuda is the State House, (right, at left with flat roof) constructed in 1620 and restored to its original state in this century. The State House was built by Governor Butler for Bermuda's Parliament and Assembly. The first Parliament was called on August 1st 1620, making Bermuda's the oldest in the British Empire due to the dissolution of the English Parliament during the Civil War (1642-47). St. Peter's Church, behind the Deliverance, was the location of this Parliament, the church being the oldest Anglican Church in continuous use in the Western Hemisphere. The first church, with a roof of Palmetto-thatch, was raised in 1612. When Parliament moved to the new capital, the State House was given to the town of St. George's and put in the trust of the freemasons who annually pay a peppercorn in rent to the Governor on the Feast of St. John the Evangelist in February.

The State House was used for a variety of purposes; the bottom floor as the House of Assembly, the middle floor as a warehouse and the top floor (no longer there, due to the restoration of the building to its original specifications) was used to store the colony's gunpowder from 1620-1772 until it was moved to Hen Island.

Surrounding the State House are Reeve Court, Bridge House, Buckingham and Casino, all owned by the Bermuda National Trust to ensure the State House's historic preservation. The National Trust owns several other buildings in St. George's and is at the forefront of efforts to preserve the town. The Trust was formed in 1970 as a watchdog of the Island's historic buildings and is also a leading environmental group, buying and preserving open space where it can and opposing some of the more environmentally unfriendly developments across the Island.

Another building in this picture owned by the National Trust is the Unfinished Church, which looks like a picturesque Gothic ruin but was in fact erected in an effort to replace St. Peter's. In 1870, the town decided that St. Peter's was beyond repair and elected to build a new church on the site of the old Government House. Work began in 1874, and soon ran into trouble when the congregation split and one faction built a church of its own. In 1883, Trinity Church in Hamilton - now the Anglican Cathedral - was burned, and its rebuilding caused a diversion of funds which might otherwise have gone to St. George's. By 1897, 21 years after the church was started, the roof was put on, but little more was done and gradually it began to disintegrate. St. Peter's was restored in the meantime and is still used.

As mentioned earlier, St. George's Parish was not divided into shares because as common property the land was supposed to pay all the administrative costs of the Bermuda Company. The 180 shareholders were limited to a maximum ten shares in the company "for the preventinge of any wrong by any sinister or undue practise". Exceptions were made to this rule and upon application a single shareholder could obtain 15 shares.

St. George's has struggled to support its people through some very harsh economic times and the St. Georgians are very independent and close in community spirit. Economic support for this end of the island has been sporadic at best, leaving the St. Georgians to fend for themselves. Almost every corner, alley and building emits the scent of the old capital's nearly four centuries of history. The buildings are special merely by the fact that that they remain true to Bermuda's architectural heritage in a concentration seen nowhere else on the Island. The town projects the sense of being in a time capsule and with care it will remain that way.

STRANDED
Howard Bay, Tucker's Town

This beach, one of 147 on the Island, has great charm and a magnificent view. Many place names on the Island change with some person's association, possession or from commonly used nicknames. Howard Bay is also known as End Beach or Turtle Bay. Turtles are protected by law as the numbers dwindled drastically in the 1900s. When Bermuda was first settled, there were thousands living around the shoreline which were quickly slaughtered, as were cahows and wild pigs. The turtle population has increased, but Taiwanese and Japanese fishing boats continue to threaten their survival as the young turtles have a hard enough time reaching the open sea. This beach was the site of attempts by Bermudian conservationist Dr. David Wingate and others to rebuild the turtle population. The immature turtles head to the Sargasso Sea, a floating platform of seaweed, where there is great protection from predators and an abundant supply of food.

Tucker's Town is named after Daniel Tucker, who as an early Governors, hoped to turn the eastern end of the Main Island into a town to compete with St.George's and St. David's. This failed and in the 1920s, the area was developed as an upscale resort for wealthy North Americans and Europeans centred on the Mid-Ocean Club and its world-class golf course. Many of the lavish residences are used only as summer homes. An early jingle about Tucker's Town reads:

All the way to Tucker's Town,	*or*	*All the way to Tucker's Town*
Four-wheel carriage rolling down,		*Drinking rum and falling down*

MAY 24th 1989
St. George's Harbour, St. George's

May 24th is Bermuda Day and the official start of summer. The first Fitted Dinghy race of the year is held on the 24th in St. George's Harbour and is always a festive occasion. Thereafter, races are held every fortnight in St. George's Harbour, Granaway Deep, or Mangrove Bay. Many avidly follow the races while others, most seen here, might choose to catch a glimpse here and there. "Raft-ups" are common during the summer and provide great opportunities for coolin' out, coolin' off and catching up with the latest "scandal". Racing in Bermuda was started by officers of the Royal Navy and British Army who introduced the sport from England. On November 1st 1844, the Bermuda Yacht Club was formed at "Moore's Calabash Tree". The club received royal patronage on December 18th 1845. In July 1882 the Royal Hamilton Amateur Dinghy Club was established by members of the R.B.Y.C. to eliminate paid crews and sail merely for the challenge. Bermuda revolutionised the sailing world with the "Bermuda Rig"which is still recognised as the most effective way to sail to windward.

Although winters are mild and the spring is warm, Bermudians traditionally wait until May 24th, which was first celebrated as Queen Victoria's birthday, before taking their first dip in the ocean. For landlubbers, May 24th is Marathon Derby day when runners take part in a half-marathon from Somerset to Hamilton. The race, which is restricted to residents, began in the early 1900s as a challenge between Masonic lodges from St. George's and Somerset. After the race, thousands of Bermudians also attend the Bermuda Day parade in Hamilton.

BERTHRIGHT
Penno's Wharf, St.George's

St.George's has always been tied to the sea and this continues to this day, with cruise ships, freighters, tall ships and yachts continuing to call at the old town.

At the beginning of the American Revolutionary War, the town was also the scene of a theft of gunpowder from Bermuda's magazine. In 1775, a group of men came ashore at Tobacco Bay and broke into the unguarded magazine where they stole the colony's stock of gunpowder. The thieves then sailed with the gunpowder to the Revolutionaries in North America. The thieves, led by some of the Island's most prominent men, engineered the theft not because they were overly sympathetic to the rebels, but because the Americans had cut off all supplies of food to the colony. During the theft, the conspirators saw a man in uniform approaching the magazine and killed him, burying him in the grounds of what was then Government House. The next day, the disappearance of a French officer being held prisoner on the Island was reported, and some 100 years later, when the grounds were being dug up for the foundations of the Unfinished Church a skeleton in French uniform was found.

The theft ensured that Bermuda would receive food supplies, but the Island was later used as a base for loyalist privateers and the Continental Congress decided to capture it. A fleet of warships was sent but it was beaten to the Island by several hours by a battalion of British troops sent to ensure the Bermudians loyalty, thus "the invasion" was thwarted.

St. George's lost most of its importance and trade when the capital was moved, but in 1861, the American Civil War broke out and with it came the Union's blockade of Southern ports. St. George's boomed as the price of cotton in Europe soared and Southern demand for armaments, munitions and manufactured goods increased as their northern supplies were cut. Blockade runners, who could slip through the northern blockade with cotton and return with European goods made a fortune and St. George's buzzed with these sleek runners and both Northern and Southern warships. Many Bermudians made fortunes in these years, and the house to the left of the tall ship in this picture, Edgewater, was built out of the proceeds of the war by a wealthy merchant.

With the end of the war, the boom ended and St.George's went into decline. Its ensuing poverty may be the inspiration for a couplet about the town which runs:

"The St. George's people are so poor,
They see you coming an' they lam the door."

The story behind Penno's Wharf is well told in Bermuda Journey: "When the Civil War began, Penno was stationed at St. George's in the Ordinance Department. He foresaw a boom and acquired this waterfront property on which he built the long, massive warehouse, one of the largest in Bermuda. Through the years of the war, Penno's Stores were packed with strange merchandise - bales of cotton from the South headed for Merseyside, and munitions of war from Europe waiting for blockade runners to load up for the dash to Charleston or Wilmington.

"Since those days the warehouse has seldom been full, but during the prohibition experiment in the United States, there were, at times, thousands of cases of liquor in Penno's Stores."

STRING ALONG

Penno's Wharf, St.George's

Many yachts travel through Bermuda, whether as a convenient mid-ocean oasis to prepare for the journey North, South, East or West or as the destination of races - the Newport - Bermuda, Annapolis - Bermuda or Marion - Bermuda. It is a great way for migrating mariners to see the Island and spread the word, while young Bermudians benefit from spare berths that allow them to venture abroad, thereby learning and perpetuating our unique maritime heritage. "Vadura" with skipper David was heading South as we stopped to chat before continuing to see "Endeavour", one of the famous J boats, depart St.George's on its maiden voyage after a complete restoration. As it happened, a friend on our boat who was visiting from Tennessee recognized "Vadura" as the yacht that helped his yacht, when it ran into difficulty in the Pacific Ocean! He subsequently sailed to the West Indies aboard the yacht.

TUCKED IN

Tucker's Town, St.George's

Butteries are a common architectural feature in Bermuda. They are either incorporated into the house or stand alone. Their steep roofs and thick walls kept meat and food fresh before the days of refrigeration. Butteries now have a wide variety of uses, including providing magnificent views as this one does at Caliban, overlooking Winsor Beach. One of Bermuda's oldest and best known butteries is located at Springfield in Sandys, where the ball on top of the buttery was blown off in a storm, but curiously did not break.

SHORE IN WINDOW
Winsor Beach, Tucker's Town

Sometimes one is fortunate to observe other peoples uses and appreciation of the many and varied beauty spots on Bermuda's face (without being spotted yourself). This Tucker's Town beach has two names - officially it is called Surf Bay, but it is often called Winsor Beach after the home at its western end.

RAINBOWS
Castle Harbour, St.George's

This unusual cloud bank shows the diversity of Bermuda's weather. Most Bermudians are weather "experts" who always have the backup of "well on this Island, anything can happen" and "don't worry, the sun will come out tomorrow". In the background at left is Cooper's Island, now part of the landfilled US base. The majority of the remaining cahows nest near Cooper's Island, where the Americans recently planned to put a baseball diamond. The lights would have caused the nocturnal birds to batter themselves to death.

The island had an area of 77.5 acres and was probably named after William Cooper of Southwark, London, a shareholder of the Somers Island Company. When Christopher Carter, Chard and Waters were left in Bermuda, they discovered 80 pounds of ambergris, then a valuable commodity, which they planned to smuggle to England. Carter revealed the conspiracy and was offered St. David's Island as a reward, but chose Cooper's . It is thought that he made his choice due to the legend of Spanish gold buried on the island. Apparently Carter did much digging, to no avail. However, "An old Bermuda tradition asserts that in 1726 a great treasure hoard of golden tankards and jewellery and doubloons was at length unearthed on Cooper's Island and that the whole cache was taken stealthily to England and disposed of as privateers' prize goods." (Terry Tucker)

NATURAL ARCHES
Natural Arches Beach, Tucker's Town

The Natural Arches in Tucker's Town is an example of a collapsed cave formed during the Ice Age where one part of the cave's roof has stayed firm to create a natural arch. It is now a popular spot for tourists and one of the most photographed scenes in Bermuda. During the storm surge of Hurricane Gabrielle in 1989 the beach disappeared, leaving nothing but the underlying rocks exposed. The storm surge churns the sand on the seabed for the duration of the storm. The sand quickly settles leaving time to deposit the fine pink granules back on the beaches.

RUNNING WILD
Mid-Ocean Beach, Tucker's Town

Hurricane Lily's storm surge 1990. The beaches along the South Shore erode annually with regular winter storms, however, all manage to recover in time for the Longtails' arrival, signalling the start of spring.
Bermudians "over-engineer" their houses to withstand the forces of hurricanes, resulting in less severe damage than in other countries. This is proven by the number of very old houses on the Island that have survived through centuries of fierce storms. The history behind many of the houses has been preserved and handed down through the years as they have often been owned by the same family since they were built. Construction of the houses is deceptively simple, but they were designed to have good ventilation and cross breezes and many have a chimney on their southeast corner to anchor the house in hurricanes. The houses have been added on to over the years, giving them a rambling appearance. The roofs are made of a double layer of brittle Bermuda stone, which is cement plastered, then limewashed. The lime purifies the rainwater - caught on the roofs and this is then stored in tanks underneath the house.

SNAKES AND LADDERS
Mullet Bay, St. George's

Now the approach road to the town of St. George's, Mullet Bay Road weaves its way around the shoreline. Cyclists have plenty of competition on Bermuda's 125 public and 125 private estate roads. 1989 recorded almost 19,000 private cars, 22,000 motorcycles and mopeds, 3,000 trucks and more than 1,500 other vehicles on the roads. Forty-five thousand vehicles is far in excess of predictions made when private cars were first permitted in 1946.

A long struggle preceded the introduction of cars because until then, virtually all transport was by carriage, bicycle or the railway which was built in the 1930s. The arrival of the US forces to build their bases in the Second World War brought military vehicles to the roads and this effectively signalled the end for the anti-car lobby, supported though it was by Woodrow Wilson, James Thurber and other frequent visitors. Even when the legislature introduced cars, the majority of Bermudians were opposed. As one dissident Assembly member said, Bermuda had "joined the great commonplace". The Government has strictly controlled maximum width, length and power for vehicles since, and has also enforced a 25 mile per hour speed limit. Residents are limited to one car per household.

WATERTOWER
John Smith's Bay, Smith's

One of the more popular beaches for locals, it is also well used by our visitors. The beach may have been named after Captain John Smith, an explorer who in 1631 produced a map of Bermuda, although he never set foot on the island. Captain Smith is a familiar name to Americans as one of the original settlers of Jamestown in 1603 who was President of the Council while Newport returned to England for supplies. He was saved by the Indian princess Pocahontas when he was about to be executed by her tribe. Pocahontas would later marry one of the survivors of the Sea Venture, John Rolfe. Rolfe and his first wife were the parents of the first child born in Bermuda and named her after the Island. Rolfe's marriage to Pocahontas ended in tragedy after he took her back to England where she died after contracting pneumonia. Rolfe is also remembered for inventing a method for curing tobacco, which enabled it to be shipped to England for sale.

Smith's Parish was named after Sir Thomas Smith, mentioned earlier. Sir Thomas had been imprisoned prior to King James' succession because he was thought to have been involved in a plot by the Earl of Essex to put a strict Protestant on the throne by force. The Earl visited Sir Thomas but not in connection with the plot. King James released Sir Thomas after knighting him in the Tower of London! Sir Thomas was greatly favoured by the King and was the Governor of the East India Company for several years, Governor of the Muscovy, Levant, French and Virginia Companies and Ambassador to the Tzar of Russia. He was the greatest shipping magnate of his day.

All the parishes except St. George's had nicknames and Smith's was known as Harris Bay. Some people still refer to the Devil's Hole area by this name. The rhyme for Smith's was :

All the way 'round Harrington Sound,
One wheel carriage rolling round.

This was a derogatory reference to the appalling state of the Parish's roads, which were only wide enough to push a wheelbarrow over.

WINTER CATCH
Watch Hill Park, Smith's

Almost every corner in Bermuda hides a scene of stunning beauty which can surprise even the most discriminating eye. A winter evening such as this is very special - the Island has a relaxed and comfortable air when it reverts to the locals after a summer of tourists, visitors, countless activities, sports and a rash of social events. The hill may have been used as lookouts for incoming ships. Watch houses served as jails for prowlers found wandering at night.

SOLITARY CONFINEMENT
Castle Harbour Golf Course, Tucker's Town

This wooded hillside with only one building visible is a rare sight in Bermuda with its population of 3,000 people per square mile. At the present rate of development, this scene will cease to be one of solitary confinement. There are eight golf courses on the island - more per square mile than anywhere else. Bermuda has more things per square mile than most places and perhaps Mark Twain was right when he said that this is "the biggest small place in the world". He would probably be amused to see how much bigger it is now, while it still retains landscapes like this.

GRAVESTONE
Harrington Sound, Hamilton Parish

This rock in Harrington Sound is near Church Bay, named for the parish church of Hamilton Parish, Holy Trinity, which can be seen in the background. The church was originally built in 1623 and subsequently added to in the 1700s and 1800s and has one of the most spectacular and romantic settings of all churches island-wide. Harrington Sound derives its name from Lucy, Countess of Bedford, who was a daughter of the first Baron Harington. The eccentric Lucy was one of the largest shareholders of the Bermuda Company and Hamilton Parish was originally named Bedford after her. She sold her shares soon after the founding of the company and was one of the few that realised a profit from the venture.

The parish was then named after the 2nd Marquis of Hamilton who was married to KingJames' daughter, Elizabeth and came down with the King from Scotland. "It was generally believed that King James's last days had been greatly saddened by the recent death of the Marquis of Hamilton, who had been one of his closest friends and the Lord Steward of his household" and considered "the gallantest gentleman of both nations" (Wilkinson). This area is known as Bailey's Bay and the 19th Century ditty goes:
"All the way to Bailey's Bay,
Fish and Taters every day."

Bailey's Bay is a place name which has survived since the 17th Century and refers to the eastern end of Hamilton Parish. The bay is one of many safe anchorages for fishermen along the coastline in the parish, which was a major shipbuilding centre during the 18th and early 19th Centuries. It was also a hive of social activity before the days of the motor car or the railway because of its relative isolation from Hamilton. But its isolation meant it also went through some periods of poverty and this may be the reason for the old jingle. Codfish and potatoes is the traditional breakfast on Sunday mornings in many Bermudian homes today, but in the days before refrigeration and at times when Bermudians were considerably poorer, salt cod from Newfoundland and potatoes were a daily staple.

LOVER'S LAKE
Ferry Reach, St. George's

It is unclear why this is called Lover's Lake but not hard to understand. The surrounding area is a Government Park and it is sad to see that today's lovers have no trees to sit underneath. A forest of endemic cedars, palmettos and olivewood certainly wouldn't go amiss.

Lover's Lake caused the deaths of members of the 2nd Battalion, Queen's Royal Rifles who camped beside it to isolate themselves from the Yellow Fever epidemic of 1864. Unbeknownst to them, or anyone else, the disease was carried by mosquitoes which bred in still water. The lake was a perfect breeding ground and its victims were subsequently buried nearby in a small cemetery.

WITHIN REACH
Ferry Reach, St. George's

Ferry Reach, at the western end of St. George's Island, refers to the reach on the south side of Ferry Island and Ferry Point. Before the causeway was built in 1871 to connect Main Island with St. George's Island, this was the thoroughfare between the islands. A small wooden bridge was built between Ferry Point and Ferry Island and a more substantial one between Main Island and Coney Island allowed the last 100 feet to be crossed with relative ease. At right are the remains of the ferry dock which was re-used temporarily after the hurricane of 1899 destroyed a large part of the Causeway. At its peak the ferry transported 600 to 800 people per day - quite a staggering number for the time.

At left are the remains of the railway which operated here from 1938 until its unfortunate demise in 1955. Many locals can still remember the railway winding its spectacularly scenic route through the Island. Many also think it a shame that it ceased to operate, and perhaps it is time to contemplate resurrecting the railway in some form (perhaps a monorail) before the trails disappear.

In the background directly behind the railway tracks is the Martello Tower which was built in 1823.

Rogue Island (top right) is where a ship's mutinous crew is supposed to have been buried after they were sentenced to death. The island also belonged to a man named Rogue.

Ferry Reach is the location of power boat racing and is one of only three stretches of water where a speed limit of more than 5 knots is permitted within 300 feet of the shore.

HOURGLASS ISLAND
Coney Island, St. George's

The name for Coney Island comes from the Coney fish which was obviously in abundant supply when Bermuda was first settled.

There were lime kilns and salt pans on the 14.5 acre island which date back to the earliest settlers. The ruins of a lime kiln remain on the south side of the island and the buildings at the northeastern end were once used as a quarantine station. They are now used as the quarters for the Department of Agriculture and Fisheries marine wardens. This beautiful island with its natural isthmus is presently being ruined by a motocross track and the spectators' lack of respect for its environmental delicacy. It seems a little ridiculous that on an island where there is a speed limit of 32 km/h that scrambling is allowed to destroy valuable and potentially beautiful parkland.

"I grew up in Bailey's Bay and I can remember when the little pool on Coney Island had seven big parrot fish in it - they certainly seemed big at the time. They were my biggest challenge and I tried my best to catch them using a variety of bait - but to no avail. Within a year of the scrambling track being established the parrot fish were replaced with refuse - what a trade! Recently I went to Coney Island to photograph the isthmus and the refuse was still there." (Ian Macdonald - Smith)

THE CABBAGE PATCH
Walsingham, Hamilton Parish

One of the aims of the Bermuda Company's founders was to develop tobacco growing in the settlement. Tobacco was still a relatively new discovery for Europeans and was in great demand. Like Virginia, Bermuda had a good climate for the crop and from early on tobacco was exported to Europe, earning sufficient money in return to purchase the goods it needed. But Bermuda could never produce tobacco of sufficient quality or quantity to compete with Virginia and by the end of the 1600s, the industry had ceased.

SOUNDING BOARD
Abbott's Cliff, Harrington Sound, Hamilton Parish

This double panorama shows all of Harrington Sound except Church Bay. Abbott's Cliff is the highest on the island and is named after Sir Maurice Abbott who was a Governor of the East India Company. On the left is Hall's Island, probably named for Thomas Hall, an early character who was part owner of the "Amity", a notorious 17th Century privateering sloop whose story is best told in William Zuill's "Bermuda Journey". The far shoreline leads round to Devil's Hole, which is a pool that has been a curiosity since 1830 when the owner Mr. Trott decided to build a wall around it to protect his livestock from poachers. In 1843 he started charging admission to those who were curious and Devil's Hole is still a tourist attraction today with a variety of fish, turtles and sharks.

The first island we see in the group on the right is Crow Island, and to the right of this is Trunk Island, which has had the same name since the Island's earliest days. There are two houses on the island, the bigger being built in 1880 by Augustus Musson, whose dream it was to spend his retirement on the Island. Mr. Musson's wife didn't want to move into the house but eventually resigned herself to it in exchange for a trip to Europe. But before the move, she died so Mr. Musson lived out his life in relative solitude on the island. To the right of Trunk Island is Rabbit Island, leased to the National Trust by Dr.W.E.Tucker. Rabbit Island was known as Collins Island, probably after Thomas Collins who owned shares in Hamilton Parish 300 years ago. The island is now a longtail sanctuary. Directly above the head of Rabbit Island is the entrance to Harrington Sound and Flatts Bridge is just visible. There were plans to cut a channel into Harrington Sound to allow the Royal Navy a safe and protected harbour. This plan was rejected in favour of the present Dockyard.

HOME AND DRY
Wilkinson Avenue, Bailey's Bay

William Wilkinson was one of the "triumvirate governors" of 1644. This was one of the most confusing periods of Bermuda's history - the English Civil War of 1642-47. Wilkinson advocated independence from the Bermuda Company and was imprisoned. He was later released and subsequently became Captain of the Castle. Palmetto fronds, at left, were used to thatch roofs before slate was used. Baskets and hats were also made from the fronds and "the soft top thereof...when roasted was like fried melons and when sod like cabbages". (William Strachey)

TRACK DOWN
Church Bay, Bailey's Bay

From the earliest days of settlement, Bermudians knew that the Island could never produce sufficient food to support its population and turned to the sea as traders. Throughout the 18th and early 19th Centuries, the salt trade was the mainstay of the economy while other Bermudians continued to work the land to produce basic foodstuffs. Arrowroot became Bermuda's next cash crop in the 1830s after the failure of tobacco 150 years earlier. The deep roots were difficult to harvest but with the exception of winter (January to March) the plants grew despite droughts, salt spray and storms. The starchy root was milled to produce a milk that was then dried and exported to England. The resurgence of agriculture in the 1830s was directly linked to the decline in Bermuda's maritime activity and when Governor Sir William Reid arrived in 1839, there were just three ploughs.

SPIT ON

Spittal Pond, Smith's

This is the same rock that is featured on page 3 of "Bermuda Through the Camera of James B. Heyl 1868-1897". Today it is difficult to imagine the trials and tribulations Heyl went through to obtain his photographs. They were made using the set-plate process where "the plates had to be prepared for exposure, and developed on the scene of action. That meant the packing and transportation of many cumbersome articles".

"In addition to the camera, there were several plate holders, each containing twelve plates - a necessary precaution against the risk of breakage. There were also two box-like affairs: the bath, (18 inches x 12 inches) and the tent (5 feet long x 5 feet wide)... In addition, there was a formidable array of bottles, containing the chemicals used in preparing the plate beforehand, and in developing and fixing it after exposure. Lastly, a five gallon water container was fitted into place on a small cart, specially contstructed for safe transport. Jessie, a gentle, sure footed grey donkey, took this cart safely over the roughest hills.

"With his head under the curtains of the tent...he coated the plate thinly with collodion - a compound consisting of gun-cotton dissolved in alcohol, with the addition of ether, and some soluble iodine or bromide salt. The coating was allowed to set, then the plate was immersed in a solution of silver nitrate, where it was allowed to remain to a minute. Silver nitrate was formed in the pores of the collodion, rendering the plate sensitive and ready for exposure."

Anyway this is Jeffrey standing on the rock to put a little perspective on the situation. Like Heyl's, this photograph is taken from Jeffrey's Hole, which is named for a runaway slave who took refuge here. Searches for him failed and it was assumed that he had escaped from the Island by boat.

Several weeks later, his master saw a 15-year-old girl disappear at sunset every day with a package under her arm. The master followed her through Spittal Pond and returned the next day with a friend. They found Jeffrey sleeping in the cave.

PONDERING

Spittal Pond, Smith's

A twenty-four acre nature reserve owned by the National Trust is truly one of Bermuda's gems, with two ponds, a natural swimming pool, a natural checkerboard, rugged coastline and the earliest graffiti on the Island. Spanish Rock bears the inscripion T F 1543. Spain claimed the islands, by right of discovery, shortly after the discovery of the American continent, and used them only as a landmark either homeward bound or from Spain, they followed the Gulf Stream to lattitude 33 degrees before laying an easterly course to the Azores.

The pond is the nesting site of herons, egrets and a few vagrant flamingoes, and all enjoying this land are asked not to disturb the wildlife or enter the fenced off areas.

The name Spittal has no definite origin, but in Bermuda Journey, Will Zuill suggests "there is a Spittal in Yorkshire, mentioned in Cobbett's Rural Rides, which may possibly furnish a clue." At two points the pond comes very close to the shoreline and during storms the eastern point is virtually connected with the sea - another possible explanation.

Recent research on Spanish Rock suggests it was not left by the Spanish, but by the Portuguese. In 1543, a Portuguese ship was wrecked off the Island and its 32 crew were stranded here for several months. TF may originally have been RP, which stands for Rex Portugaline. A cross at the same location is probably the badge of the Portuguese Order of Christ. The carving was perhaps by a member of the ship's company, as he kept watch for a ship which could rescue the crew. The carving no longer exists, but a brass casting has been put in its place.

The National Trust is in the process of replanting Spittal Pond with endemic trees, but work is slow because of the reliance on volunteer help and a lack of funds. Land rich and cash poor, the Trust valiantly struggles to purchase, restore and preserve properties of intrinsic value to our island. Unfortunately the work done by the Trust is not always fully appreciated or supported. It will be a shame if future generations look back on things lost forever because too few cared.

PLOT TO KILL
Pokiok Farm, Smith's

It is a pity to think that in a few years this lovely piece of farmland may go the way of most of the rest - developed - out of economic necessity and a corresponding lack of Government and public support and incentive for landowners to preserve the few remaining "large" areas of open space in Bermuda.

SPRING'S CLEAN UP
Palmetto Bay Hotel, Flatts Village

Palmetto Bay Hotel, shown here, is one of many charming Bermudian homes converted for use as a small hotel. There are a few varieties of annual trees -poinciana, fiddlewood and mahogany on the property. The branch of the mahogany tree can be seen in the foreground and was planted by a merchant, Samuel Musson, in 1840 at the entrance to the house, which was then called Palmetto Grove. Mr. Musson spent his later years sitting under the shade of the tree with a jug of "sangaree" which he happily shared with his friends as they passed by. It was, by all accounts, a popular stopping place.

The easter lilies in the foreground are reminders of what was once a major export on the Island in the Nineteenth and early Twentieth Centuries. Lily bulbs grew extremely well in Bermuda, and many of Bermuda's fields were planted with them. Mr. Howard Smith of St. David's Island was responsible for creating his own strain of Easter Lily, Howardii, and this has become the Island's most durable strain. The Perfume Factory in Bailey's Bay produces its own perfume from the lilies' petals.

Mark Twain immortalised this mahogany tree when he visited the Island and noted that there was one mahogany tree in Bermuda and that he counted it every time he passed. Sir John Cox (1900-90), Speaker of the House, was passing Palmetto Bay after a hurricane in the 1930s and saw Bermuda Electric Light Co. employees cutting a damaged bough from the tree. He asked them to deliver the bough to his residence, The Grove in Devonshire, where it was turned into two display cabinets for Sir John's extensive fan collection.

In 1895, the house was the residence of Archdeacon Tucker, the Island's leading churchman of the time, and it was here that the first meeting of the Bermuda Historical Society took place as the Archdeacon wanted to stimulate interest in local history.

VERDMONT
Collector's Hill, Smith's

Verdmont, perhaps the National Trust's best museum, is a fine example of a 17th Century mansion. Verdmont, French for Green Hill, may be derived from John Green, an American loyalist who came to Bermuda at the end of the Revolutionary War and became a judge in the Court of Vice Admiralty, which had responsibility for deciding whether ships taken by the Royal Navy and privateers were legitimate prizes. As a judge he developed a fearsome reputation among Americans because he treated them with the utmost severity. "The pretext for the ruthless condemnation of American ships was always the same," says William Zuill in Bermuda Journey, " - that they were trading with France, who was at war with Britain - and evidence to the contrary was seldom acccepted. Thus it came to be accepted that any American ship taken into Bermuda was a complete loss, and it was declared that Judge Green showed no mercy. With such encouragement from the court, privateering for a time became Bermuda's chief industry." It is also thought that the severity of Green's judgements may have contributed to the outbreak of the War of 1812.

The house was the home of early Collectors of Customs, hence the name Collector's Hill. It also has an unusual double roof containing an attic with one small window overlooking the South Shore, traditionally the main approach to the Island for ships. Another curious feature of the house is the door, which is out of symmetry with the rest of the facade. It is thought that the house was originally a wooden structure and the stone walls were later built around the old frame. It seems the original hand-carved cedar staircase was retained and the door moved to the left, sacrificing aesthetics in the process.

RAINCOAT

OLD BOUNDARY

PLAIN TO SEE

DARK CLOUD LOOMING

DEFORESTATION SEA

THE PAMPAS

Raincoats may be needed when the next generation cries about the subdvision of the Pampas and its potential metamorphosis into something similar to the hillside under the rainbow opposite. The Pampas could become part of a coastal park running from John Smith's Bay through Spittal Pond, Pokiok Farm and all the way to Devonshire Bay.

The Pampas has already been subdivided, but a compromise with the owners, or a Government method of compensating landowners for not developing their open land, could preserve this valuable property. Until the late 1960's, there were few restrictions on building or subdivisions in Bermuda. A growing population and increasing wealth led to a building boom and a rapid reduction in the amount of open space. The Government, spurred by environmental groups like the National Trust and later Save Open Spaces, has imposed restrictions on both development and land division but will have to do more in the future to retain what is left of the Island's rural charm and open space.

This year a commission of inquiry into Bermuda's marine environment had several sensible suggestions about how the Island's environment could be safeguarded "through the development and use of parks, including marine parks and by seeking the co-operation of non-governmental organisations."

The Commission also recommended that a Department of the Environment be established with responsibility for environmental planning. Such a department would cut down on the amount of time Government has to spend dealing with environmental crises as has often been the case in the past.

Government has yet to reply to the Commission's recommendations or introduce a new development plan. It is hoped that provision will be made for the Pampas and that we will save this space.

WISTFUL

Flatts Village, Hamilton

Wistowe, on the North Shore Road outside of Flatts, is about 250 years old and was named by a rector in remembrance of his curacy in the town of Wistowe, England. It has been a theatre, a roadhouse, a beauty shop and a bakery. As a bakery, it supplied naval ships anchored off the North Shore with bread. Around the same time, a narrow canal was cut through the property to join Harrington Sound with the Flatts to provide water power for grinding aloes. The aloe's juice was used to cure dysentery by the British forces in the War of 1812.

Wistowe was also the location of a famous duel in 1840. At a dance and dinner party at the house, two men, one newly arrived and married to a local belle, fell into a disagreement - possibly over the bride - which ended with the new arrival, Peter Nice, slapping Robert Hill. Both men immediately drew swords and prepared to fight it out on the spot, but other guests intervened, saying "Not here, gentlemen - ladies are present."

The two men withdrew to the waterside and duelled with swords. After just a few passes, Hill struck Nice in the stomach, giving him a mortal wound of which he died the next day. Hill threw his sword to the ground and declared: "You see gentlemen, I did it in self-defence." He then surrendered to an officer standing among the spectators and was arrested. At his trial, he was convicted of murder and sentenced to death, but the Governor suspended the sentence pending an appeal to the King. Many weeks later, a vessel arrived from England with a full pardon for Hill.

Later, the house would be occupied by Professor Reginald Fessenden, who invented voice radio and married a Bermudian. He thought the coconut trees in the garden should bear more fruit, and hired a West Indian who called himself the "cocoa-tree doctor" to assist him. The "doctor" climbed to the top of the trees and showered the budding fruit with salt. The resulting crop was better than ever before.

FISHFINGERS
Penhurst Park, Smith's

This exceptional summer sunset was captured at Penhurst Park while this family caught its "greaze" or dinner! Penhurst was owned by an old Bermuda family, thePenistons, and this was their "hurst", or hill.

ON THE RIGHT TRACK
Devonshire Bay, Devonshire

This palmetto lined drive is in Devonshire Parish, which was named for the Adventurer William, Lord Cavendish, who became the Earl of Devonshire after the seat became vacant - and after he contributed 10,000 pounds for one of King James' hunting expeditions. He died of the plague in 1628. Just to the west of Devonshire Bay is the site of Bermuda's only enemy landing.

"A few days before the outbreak of war, so the story goes, a German merchantman sailed out of New York harbour, and as soon as war was declared she became an armed raider. When nearing Bermuda, she stopped - far enough away to be unseen from land - and sent three men ashore in one of the ship's boats. The boat made a landing below Devonshire Fort, and one of the crew walked from there into Hamilton and posted a letter, thus proving that he had visited the island." (Bermuda Journey)

As previously mentioned palmettos were used for food and shelter but a little known use was as a drink. The sap of the palmetto was fermented, producing "bibby", a very strong alcoholic beverage which was quickly made illegal. The palmetto became very scarce during the latter part of last century and it is refreshing now to see its resurgence throughout the Island.

CURRENT SITUATION
Flatts Village

Flatts Village is a "sleepy little place", which has not changed much over the centuries.

"The origin of the name Flatts is obscure. Some have tried to find a connection with the shallow water in the channel, but this is not satisfactory when one recalls that the ocean-going ships used the harbour. Not long ago a seventeenth century deed turned up in which the name was spelled Fleighst. This is not in the Oxford Dictionary but there is "fleigh", an obsolete form of "flake", meaning a stage or frame for drying fish, which seems to be a promising clue.

"Like Crow Lane (Hamilton Harbour), Riddell's Bay, Ely's Harbour and Mangrove Bay, Flatts was one of the earliest settlements because all communications were by boat and these little harbours became natural centres for trade. Later when Bermudians turned to shipbuilding and overseas trading, these villages took on the significance of home ports." (Bermuda Journey)

The boat "Iridio" in the foreground belongs to the Bermuda Aquarium, one of Bermuda's prime scientific centres. The Aquarium features almost all of the Island's marine creatures and this collection is frequently supplemented. It also has a zoo and a natural history museum. The boat was an old Bermuda sloop (its sleek sailing lines reveal its origins) that has been converted for more practical use.

At right, St. James' Court can just be seen. This is a condominium development that was built in 1985-6 on the site of the old Frascati and the Coral Island Hotel. This is the site of the first Bermuda Biological Station, established in 1903 as a joint venture between Bermuda and two US universities (Harvard and New York) to study the Island's ecology. To the left of this photograph is Flatts Bridge which, along with Coney Island Bridge and Somerset Bridge, was one of the first to link the islands together. The tide which can be seen flowing out proves troublesome to boaters trying to get through the contraflow.

FORESTALL
Brighton Hill, Devonshire

This hillside provides a hint of what Bermuda once looked like and gives a taste of what Bermuda can be again. This is one of the few cedar forests on the Island. The indigenous Bermuda cedar is difficult to germinate and grow. The Island was originally carpeted in a forest of massive cedars, palmettos and olivewood. The forests supported sparrows, robins, woodpeckers and crows while the coastline hosted grey and white herons, ducks, pimlicoes, castle boobies, sand birds, hawks, longtails and cahows, according to William Strachey in his account of the shipwreck. The deforestation of Bermuda began immediately, with the wood being used as the primary house and ship building material.

By the early 1800s there was barely a cedar tree to be seen. The demand for the wood was immense as its superiority became apparent to mariners. The wood, though brittle, is light and incredibly resistant to the elements. Around 1810 Joseph Clayton Jennings sold 10,000 cedar trees for 2,500 pounds - or four trees per pound. The wood now fetches upwards of $35 per board foot, and then only if a seller can be found. It is now greatly cherished and used with much greater care than before.

In 1944-5 a massive blight of microscopic scale affected the remaining cedar trees; starting in Paget Parish, moving north-east initially with the prevailing winds and then affecting the rest of the island. Almost all of the trees died, leaving a landscape of barren, contorted skeletons. Bermuda finally experienced winter.

Short-term reforestation with casuarina trees became vital, with palms and bay grapes also filling the gaps. It has taken 50 years for the cedar trees to start re-establishing themselves in any number, due to the dilligence of many individuals in the community who refused to allow the cedar tree to die out. The casuarina tree has done great service to Bermuda but the time has come to reforest with cedars wherever possible so that in 50 years time the landscape is recarpeted. Hurricane Emily helped clear space for replanting by felling many of the shallow rooted casuarinas.

Winter is almost over, spring is in the air and summer is overdue.

SHELL OUT
Shelly Bay, Hamilton Parish

"Shelly Bay was named for Henry Shelly, one of the Sea Venture company, who discovered it "swarming with mullets and excellent pilchards". It lies near the (former) race track and is the longest beach on the North Shore. In early times, sand and the marsh extended nearly to the end of the point, and at one place the old road to St. George's crossed this low lying land. But the creepers and plants on the shore were destroyed and this loosened the sand and laid it open to encroachment, with the result that the sea thrust inland for a considerable distance. The line of the old road, now submerged, can be seen clearly on a calm day." (Bermuda Journey)

The house in the background, Bowen House, although recently built, has great Bermudian features that allow some modern touches to blend in well. The roof is more traditional than most Bermudian houses with dowelled rafters which allow the roof to give and will outlast any of today's modern roofs.

MOTHER SUPERIOR
Shelly Bay, Hamilton Parish

The beach is ideal for children and the water stays shallow for a considerable distance. The "Dish" is a constant reminder of the battle between progress and nature. This shot demonstrates the environmental conflict on the Island - everyone wants "a piece of the rock". Within the last five years there has been a rash of condominium developments which have taken much of the strain off the development of our open spaces.

Childhood here is very special in a safe community with great sandpits and splashpools. There is a beach close to almost everyone. Special events for children throughout the year at the Agricultural Show and camps in the summer, teach various skills, values and help them appreciate their heritage.

NORTH FOLK PINE FOR
Shelly Bay, Hamilton Parish

Fairhaven is a charming example of Victorian architecture. Norfolk pines were widely planted as part of the effort to reforest Bermuda after the cedar blight.

MIDNIGHT BLUES
Hungry Bay, Paget

The name Hungry Bay has uncertain origins, although William Zuill in Bermuda Journey seemed to think that there were two possibilities - "the name is said to come from the belief that the sea encroached more at this spot than elsewhere; another possible explanation is that the moan of the sea on the breaker outside the bay, which is often heard before rain, was likened to the roar of a hungry animal."

Hungry Bay is now a very quiet place, protected by mangroves and almost as picturesque as it was in 1609. The bay has drawn very little attention to itself but in 1860 it became famous as this article from the Royal Gazette shows:

SEA SERPENT ASHORE. On Sunday noon a creature came ashore at Hungry Bay which promises to play a part in the Natural History of the World. In fact it is in no spirit of exaggeration that we venture to characterise it as a key to the marvellous and hitherto discredited accounts which many travellers have given of the appearance of Sea Serpents.

The animal in question rushed ashore making a loud, rustling noise which greatly surprised a gentleman who happened to be in the neighbourhood and who immediately repaired to the spot whence the sound came. Here he discovered a creature which familiar as he was with all forms of marine zoology which swarm our coasts fairly took him by surprise. The animal was in length 16'9" and its form unlike that of any known fish, at least any known fish in these waters. It was broad and flat, in fact ribbon like and its motion evidently had been edge up. The animal's greatest width was about 9 inches and its greatest thickness about 4 inches. It had no fins. Its colour was a dazzling silvery white with a remarkable exception presently to be noted. It had very ample gills and was apparently not furnished with teeth. The most singular feature about this creature and perhaps the most characteristic was its mane composed of a series of filaments from two to three feet long at most and gradually diminishing towards the tail, all the filaments very fine and tapering and all of a bright scarlet colour. It is obvious that as the animal worked its way through the water with the aid of its Archimedean screw tail, this set of appendages would exactly answer the description and portraiture of the main described by many travellers."

The bones of this fish, now thought to be an oarfish, were sent to the British Museum. In May 1991, an incomplete example of the same species was found on Challenger Bank, 30 miles southwest of Bermuda.

CONCORDIA
Camden Hill, Paget

Overlooking the Botanical Gardens, the Tucker family property and Hungry Bay permitted this timely shot with racy cloud. There is now a house to the left of those shown and sadly the old stone wall has been cut off. Paget Parish was named for William, 4th Lord Paget who was the executor for Lord Harington and also cousin of Lord De la Warr, the first Governor of the Virginia Colony. Paget, who had 10 shares in the Bermuda Company, was liked by the colonists and died in 1629. The old name for the Paget area was Crow Lane, where there was a concentration of wealthy families and the ditty by which it is remembered goes like this:

"All the way to Crow Lane side
Nothing there but foolish pride."

POINTING FINGERS
Point Finger Road, Paget

Point Finger Road, originally called Finger Point Road, developed as a track connecting the City of Hamilton with South Shore Road, then the only road through the whole of Bermuda. A large wooden sign with a pointing finger painted on it, to help travellers find their way, gave the road its name. A version of the sign still exists and was recently restored.

The road is used primarily as access to residences, the hospital and the Department of Agriculture and Fisheries. Access to the City of Hamilton from the South Shore Road is now further west via two roundabouts.

GRAPE BAY

Grape Bay has a magical quality that defies description, and its continual changes never cease to amaze. Sadly, the entrance to the bay has been destroyed by hurricanes. There are some rock formations similar to the checker board at Spittal Pond. The bay is named for the abundance of Bay Grape trees which line the beach.

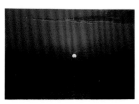

"Devonshire Dock is a picturesque little haven and the only small boat harbour on the North Shore between Spanish Point and Flatts. In times past there was a greensward gently sloping toward the cove and behind this, covering the hillside, a thick grove of cedars. The glade, open to the sea on one side and protected by the cedar grove on the other, was known as the Dock Bottom, and for a short period this romantic spot became a rendezvous for the young folk of Devonshire.

"During the war with America in 1815 a large British fleet met at Bermuda to prepare an attack upon the city of Washington. Ships rode at anchor along the entire length of the North Shore, and at Devonshire Dock, so it is said, small craft from the vessels came and went constantly, collecting fresh vegetables and drawing water from the nearby wells.

"Before long the young sailors made friends ashore, and thus it came about that every afternoon the maidens of the parish, decorously accompanied by parents, assembled at Dock Bottom to meet the lads from the ships. Then, so the pretty narrative relates, several old gentlemen would arrive, bringing their fiddles, and play for the young people, who passed the sunny afternoon dancing on the greensward." (Bermuda Journey)

Devonshire was commonly called Brackish Pond because of the large area of marshland in the centre of the Parish and the popular verse went:

> All the way to Brackish Pond,
> Cow heel soup 'n' damaged corn.

SILVER GREY
Lane Hill, Devonshire

This view is from the eastern end of Hamilton Harbour looking west-southwest from Lane Hill with White's Island just left of centre and Hinson's Island to the right of the channel that leads to Granaway Deep. The two small islands in front of Hinson's Island are Burnt Island (left) and Doctor's Island. Lane Hill takes its name from Crow Lane Harbour at the very eastern end of Hamilton Harbour; the Lane refers to the narrow track of water.

White's Island was originally known as Hunt's Island after an early family of settlers. According to Terry Tucker in The Islands of Bermuda: "Here lived a well known family of sail makers - the Whites. Ship building also took place on this convenient island... in 1855, the Graceful Clipper barque "Pearl" (252 tonnes) built by Nathaniel Yates was launched. After several runs, her ultimate fate became one of the unsolved mysteries of the sea. In October 1858, commanded by William Smith Hutchings and with many Bermudians aboard, she sailed for the Azores... she was never heard of again.

"When William White, the sailmaker, died in 1860, every ship in the harbour flew her colours at half-mast. We still remember him in the 'popular' name of the island, though actually the White's were tenants of the Hunts.

"In the meantime, the Corporation of Hamilton had, in mid-19th century, acquired the north part of the island for landing stores. Thirty years earlier, Governor Cockburn had recommended this instead of dumping them untidily on Hamilton wharves. And by 1855, the remainder of White's was bought by the Corporation from the Hunt estate to make bathing places for that strange new importation - the winter tourist! The little island, with its new bathing huts, became a popular resort."

Hinson's Island, first named Godet's, is one of the few islands in the Great Sound to be inhabited year-round and contained permanent homes from early on.

The island is named for the Hinson family some of whom lived there in addition to owning land at Salt Kettle on the Paget shore. There were four or five generations of doctors in the family, and in 1763 one of these was one of the first to advocate preventative innoculation and quarantine for smallpox. One of his descendants, Dr. Henry Hinson, also practised architecture as a hobby and designed steeples for several of the island's churches.

The island was used as a school in 1902 for more than 200 boys who were among the prisoners of war brought to Bermuda during the Boer War. Later, Major Hal Kitchener, a veteran of World War I, would buy the island and build a home on its highest point. He and another aviator brought the first aircraft to be based in Bermuda and formed the Bermuda and West Atlantic Aviation Company. They planned to conduct surveys in Central and South America and also hoped to revive the whaling industry by spotting whales from the air.

Burnt Island may have derived its name during Governor Dan Tucker's administration when a plague of rats infested the Island. Underbrush on much of Bermuda was burnt in order to destroy their nests.

HAZY DAYS AND LAZY WAYS
Bostock Hill West, Paget

Taken on a rare hazy day, this tranquil scene brings back nostalgic visions of the romantic past, when many of the Island's inhabitants lived off the ocean. The spit of land on the left is Salt Kettle, one of the first communities on the Main Island. This was where salt was produced by evaporating seawater in pans or, as the name implies, kettles. Bermuda has sister islands east of the Bahamas, the Turks and Caicos Islands, where in 1678 Bermudians first produced salt on a commercial scale in huge settling ponds. The salt was then transported to the east coast of North America and Newfoundland where it was a valuable trading commodity. In return, food, clothing and other commodities that Bermuda needed were purchased. The business, which by 1750 directly involved 10 percent of the Island's population and saw 100,000 bushels of salt exported, was constantly threatened by the Bahamas government, pirates and enemies of Britain. In 1692 the Governor of the Bahamas, a borderline pirate, tried to tax the salt and started seizing Bermudian ships, nearly leading to war.

In 1706, the Turks were captured by the French and Spanish during the War of the Spanish Succession. The islands were restored to Bermudian control in 1710 by Captain Lewis Middleton in the privateer "Rose". By the time peace was declared in 1713 the Bahamas colony, which the French and Spanish had almost wiped out, was in the hands of pirates, among them Edward Teach, the infamous Blackbeard. Bermudians and their trade were again threatened. After failed negotiations coupled with the threat of invasion, Bermuda's rule of the Turks ceased. The Bahamas were restored to law and order by former privateer Woodes Rogers. Although Bermuda claimed sovereignty, the Turks were amalgamated with the rest of the Bahamas. The salt trade continued through the 1800's and there are still reminders of Bermuda's early influence in the Turks, including family names and some distinctive Bermudian architecture.

In the background on the left is Hinson's Island and to the right, Watling Island can just be made out. Behind Watling are Marshall's Island and Long Island.

ENISLE EIGHT
Bostock Hill West, Paget

From left to right (bottom row): Doctor's Island, skip one, Spectacle Island, hop, skip and jump to the left and the spit of land is Bluck's Island, with Long Island peeking out behind. In the distance is Lambda Island with Pearl Island to its right. On the right of the photograph are the two rocks which make up Two Rock Passage - now the main shipping channel.

Spectacle Island is actually two small islets, but a ridge at low tide gives it the shape of a pair of old-fashioned glasses - "pince-nez".

There are two houses on Bluck's Island, formerly known as Denslow's or Dyer's, one of which is turreted. The name for the island comes from Arthur William Bluck, the Mayor of Hamilton from 1913 to 1926, who bought it as a summer home. The larger house was built by William Wallace Denslow, who *illustrated "The Wonderful Wizard of Oz" and designed the sets and costumes for the stage play.*

Pearl's name may be derived from its shape, but it could also have come from the Bermuda Company's hope that the Island would be a source of pearls after early reports of oysters were received.

Early predictions of "one hundred seed pearls in each oyster" were never fulfilled, but they did lead to Richard Norwood, who would later survey the Island and divide it into tribes and shares, being sent out to engage in pearl fishing because he had invented a diving bell .

GOLD STANDARD

Bostock Hill West, Paget

Evening's arrival at the port of call! Shown is Point Shares, Pembroke with Saltus Island nestled at its base in Soncy Bay. The picture shows how 60,000 people can fit onto 21 square miles; with homes nestled into the hillsides throughout the Island. During the summer, yachts stay for extended periods, lapping up a safe haven and famous Bermudian hospitality.

Saltus is a two acre island now owned by the National Trust as a nature reserve. It was originally owned by Richard Norwood and subsequently bequeathed to a Samuel Saltus, hence the name. The most famous of Saltus' descendants, also named Samuel (1800-1880), was a merchant and ship-owner who lived at Norwood and in his will left 12,800 pounds to found a school, Saltus Grammar School. Bostock Hill is named after an early settler who emigrated to Jamaica before 1670.

TOWNSCAPE

City of Hamilton, Pembroke

Hamilton, Bermuda's capital, is also its main commercial centre and this is clear from its distinctive skyline. The town became the Island's capital in 1815 and, blessed with a safe harbour, it became the Island's major port and the Island's business centre.

This picture shows some of the city's most important buildings. In the foreground at left is the Royal Bermuda Yacht Club, where until the introduction of universal adult suffrage in 1968, it was said the Island's business leaders, comprised mainly of the Islands' oldest white families, would gather to decide the destiny of the Island. Whether this is true or not is unclear, but it is still an exclusive club which is the centre of the Island's sailing fraternity. Beside the RBYC on Albuoy's Point is the main headquarters of the Bank of Bermuda, the Island's largest bank. With branches in London, New York, the Cayman Islands, Hong Kong, Guernsey, the Isle of Man and Luxembourg, the bank symbolises the importance of international business to the Island. It is also the largest single private employer. To the right of the Bank runs Front Street, the Island's main shopping street and a magnet for tourists. Hamilton's docks run alongside Front Street and every week, freighters call here to unload their containers. In the summer, they are joined by cruise ships which tower over the street.

Three great buildings line the back of the Hamilton skyline. The City Hall, the white building at left, is the headquarters of the Corporation of Hamilton, which manages the city and also houses art galleries and a theatre. It was designed by Will Onions, one of the Island's greatest architects, and the man who formalised Bermudian vernacular architecture. Although the building was criticised when it was built, today it is recognised as an important contribution to the architecture of the Island. The tower on the building contains, not a clock, but a wind gauge and the weathervane on its top is a sailing ship, the symbol of the capital.

The large church to the right is the Anglican Cathedral which was finished in 1911 and replaced Trinity Church, which burnt to the ground in 1884 after being built only 14 years earlier.

To its right is the Sessions House, which houses the Supreme Court and the House of Assembly. It is an example of Italian inspired Victorian Colonial municipal architecture with its red brick arches.

Most retail trade on the island relies on tourist spending, and as a result fluctuations in world economies are felt here. There has been a downturn in locally made goods available in recent years and this is something many people hope to see revitalised.Hopefully this will happen soon, and talented young people will be encouraged to produce well made, creative goods.

Pembroke Parish is named for William Herbert, the 3rd Earl of Pembroke who was a great patron of literature and after whom Pembroke College, Oxford is also named. Most of the Adventurers were forceful, shrewd businessmen but according to Sir Francis Bacon, Pembroke was "for his person not effectual".

CUTTIN' SHREW
Richmond Road, City of Hamilton

The habit of cutting through the Richmond Road gas station to bypass the stop lights is not encouraged by the proprietors. The importance of international business can be seen in this Christmas scene with The Bank of Butterfield on the left and American International in the background centre. American International was the first exempted insurance company on the Island and now there are about seven thousand here. They employ about 2,000 directly on the understanding that they train more Bermudians for positions within their respective organisations. Earnings from the companies account for more than 40 percent of the Island's gross domestic product. Bermuda is attractive to the international businesses because it is politically stable, offers expertise in banking, accounting and legal facilities, has excellent communications, low taxes and a good business environment. Many of the businesses are insurance companies and the Island is an internationally recognised insurance centre. Other exempted companies are involved in financial services, ship management and commodity trading. In recent years, a number of Hong Kong-based companies, seeking a safe haven for 1997 when the Chinese take over their city, have established subsidiaries in Bermuda .

EITHER WAY
Front and Queen Streets, City of Hamilton

Front Street is a two way street in a predominantly one way traffic system in Hamilton. During rush hour in the morning police direct traffic from the "birdcage" seen with its customary Christmas hat. This is probably the most popular photo location for tourists on the Island. Many of the retail stores - but sadly, not all - decorate their facades for Christmas with locals comparing aesthetics to previous years. Victoria Block, now Gosling Brothers Front Street liquor outlet, is so called because Queen Victoria's accession to the throne was announced from this site; though the original house, which for a time was used as the custom house and council chamber, has been replaced since the 1835 proclamation. The national alcoholic beverage is the "Dark and Stormy" - Gosling's famous Black Rum and ginger beer. The rum is very smooth and is also mixed with coke, to make the "Black and Coke". To the right of Victoria Block are the Island's two major department stores, H.A.&E. Smiths and Trimingham Brothers. Buildings on Front Street must retain their distinctive characteristics under Government planning regulations, meaning they cannot increase the height and depth of their shopfronts and they must keep their verandahs, to provide a covered walkway for pedestrians and shoppers.

LIGHTHEADED
Church Street, City of Hamilton

This is the junction of Queen and Church Streets, and on Church Street are the City Hall, the Cathedral and the Sessions House which define the city's skyline. All other buildings must be lower to retain the distinctive charm of the skyline and Bermuda thus faces the dilemma of "up or out". North of the City of Hamilton is a valley which houses Pembroke Marsh and the Island's main dump. This is where a park is to be constructed, providing an opportunity to develop around the park with a combination of residential and office buildings that can be reasonably tall without intruding on the skyline. This would ease traffic congestion and also prevent any major development of remaining open space, which seems inevitable at the present rate of expansion.

THE GHOSTS OF DELIVERANCE
Albouy's Point, City of Hamilton

The Ferry Terminal is in the heart of the city with good access to the harbour and the Great Sound coastline, providing commuters with a spectacular way to get to work. Ferries have been in existence since the early 1600s and started operating in the Sound in 1794 when William Riddell & Co., started a ferry service between Salt Kettle and St.George's. This was a sailboat ferry and it ran twice a week; "one-way passage for ladies and gentlemen was 18d., for Negroes, 10d.".

"The Salt Kettle Ferry must have commenced soon after Hamilton was laid out. At first it was a service by rowboats...but by 1853, Daniel Astwood was using a sailboat, and in 1867 a small steamboat, "the Express," took up the work. The Express was regarded as such a novelty that on the first day between three and four hundred persons crossed the harbour. Many people had never been in a steamer before and enthusiastically took this opportunity to enjoy a new thrill." (Bermuda Journey)

The present day service is efficiently operated and has expanded to include Boaz Island where there is a new housing complex. The other stops are Lower Ferry, Hodgson's, Salt Kettle, Darrell's Wharf, Hinson's Island, Belmont, Somerset Bridge, Cavello Bay, Watford Bridge and the Dockyard Ferries.

DEJA VIEW
Elliot Street, City of Hamilton

A quaint city scene that has changed already. The house in the background has been obscured from view by another building and the stores have changed hands. The expansion of the city has accelerated in the last 20 years and as a result many lovely buildings, Victorian and older, have disappeared, partly because at the time of writing, no policy of designating buildings as historic landmarks exists. It is not clear when these Victorian, military-style buildings were constructed, but they are unusual for Bermuda, where most neighbouring buildings vary enormously.

WATERLOO HOUSE
Pitts Bay Road, Pembroke

This guest house is a superb example of old Bermuda architecture. The house and the surrounding area were named for the Battle of Waterloo in 1815, where Wellington defeated Napoleon and brought the Napoleonic Wars to an end after 25 years. An area in St. George's was named Wellington at the same time, commemorating the great man, rather than his final victory. Waterloo House was originally the home of Mr. Augustus Musson, one of the founding fathers of the City of Hamilton and a leading merchant of the early nineteenth century.

YELLOW LINES
Ferrars Lane, Pembroke

Ferrars Lane is named for two of the original Adventurers of Bermuda. John Ferrar was the "deputy" of the Company and during the great struggles for dominance between Parliament and the Crown in Seventeenth Century England, he administered the Company while its head, Sir Edwin Sandys, for whom Sandys Parish is named, dedicated himself to matters of state. John's brother Nicholas would later assume responsibility for the Company. In the early days of Bermuda, the Ferrars owned a large share of land in Warwick, but this must have passed out of their family's hands later. Like many of the Company's founders, the brothers never visited the remote island over which they had so much influence. This peaceful lane, a green buffer between Hamilton and the light industrial area to the north of the city, is the only physical reminder Bermuda now has of this family.

THE WESTERN FRONT
North Shore, Pembroke

Though slightly out of context, the title is appropriate as Bermuda became the "Gibraltar of the West" with the construction of Dockyard which began in 1809. The Moongate, seen top left, originates from China but has been adopted by Bermudians as an acceptable architectural feature. The Moongate is supposed to bring good luck to newlyweds who pass through it. Bermuda is a popular honeymoon destination. The name honeymoon comes from the Teutons, European warriors, who drank mead for 30 days after marriage. Mead is honey wine and 30 days is one moon hence "honeymoon". Probably the most famous Teuton, Attila the Hun, is said to have drunk so much mead at his wedding feast that he died.

TRI-CYCLISTS
Astwood Cove, Warwick

These cyclists making their way around Astwood Cove reflect the keen interest Bermudians take in virtually all sports - barring ice hockey. For an island of its size, Bermuda has many outstanding athletes, who have excelled in international competition. Soccer is the Island's most popular sport and several Bermudians have played professionally in England and North America, while professional European teams and national teams from the US and the Caribbean also tour locally. Cricket is the next most popular sport and the Island is well known for its prowess. Athletics is also popular, with Bermudians competing in the Olympic and Commonwealth Games, in which high jumper, Clarence Saunders, won a gold medal in 1990. Bermuda also hosts international sailing events, marathons and triathlons in which these athletes are competing. Bermuda also hosts the Rugby Classic for former international players in their 30s. It is an exciting event and allows Bermudians to see a world class event.

Bermudians were responsible for the introduction of tennis to the United States. In 1873 a Mr. Tom Middleton returned to Bermuda from England with the necessary equipment to play the game. However, in the Victorian era it was considered unladylike to run. Middleton spared his wife and sold the tennis gear to Mr. Gray of Clermont, Paget who built what is believed to be the first tennis court in the western hemisphere. Miss Mary Outerbridge had the Staten Island Cricket Club build a tennis court in 1874 after learning to play the game at Clermont.

COVE PARK
Astwood Cove, Warwick

Probably named for Frederick 'Gunny' Astwood, a whaler who had his shed near the cove. The road leading to the cove was the original South Shore Road while the present road was quarried to go over the hill as can be seen in Tri-cyclists. In the 1970s, Government bought the land between the new road and the beach when it was put up for sale and was zoned for a hotel development. It now maintains greenhouses and fields in the valley while the rest of the property is a public park.

HALCYON DAYS
Soncy Bay, Pembroke

This picture was taken from Halcyon, overlooking Hamilton Harbour and the Great Sound. Built in 1926, Halcyon is an architectural delight with charming quarry gardens. The tender passing in the background is the Canima, which gave noble service for many years ferrying cruise ship passengers, it was also used for "booze cruises" during College Weeks and during the summer. Named for the Island's first Atlantic passenger ship, she was sold in 1989 to a Canadian shipping firm and is already sadly missed.

CASUAL OBSERVATION

Spectacle Island, The Great Sound

Cup Match! Everyone waits for Cup Match, a two day cricket match between St. George's and Somerset which is the most popular Public Holiday of the year. The game is always on the Thursday and Friday of the weekend nearest August 1, and was started to commemorate the abolition of slavery in 1834. So many people took time off work to see the match that eventually it was declared a public holiday. Explaining the game of cricket to the uninitiated is a confusion of "ins" and "outs". "The Game" is a great social occasion and the scene of much banter and light-hearted inter-parish taunts. In earlier times the match was one of the only times in the year that residents of the extreme parishes interacted. Cup Match is the location of "the Stock market" which is a tent with "Crown and Anchor" tables. "Hook and Hat", as it is commonly called, is an old Royal Navy dice game and Cup Match is the one of the few times when public gambling is allowed.

Many residents take the opportunity to camp in parks or on one of the islands in the Great Sound over the four day holiday. The camps in the Great Sound have such witty names as The Bomb Shelter, Camp Crucial, Camp Ping (seen here), Camp Safely, Camp Serious, Camp Space and Camp Tuch Dis. Inevitably many "spectacles" transpire during the holiday.

DI-SOLUTION   RESURRECTION

Belmont, Warwick

Hurricane Emily ravaged Bermuda on September 27th, 1987. Di-solution was taken immediately after the hurricane and Resurrection after the recovery began. Much of Bermuda's treeline was destroyed in a mere hour, opening up views and revealing houses that many never knew existed.

Though it will take many years to return to its old state, the rate of recovery is faster than anyone (even the optimists!) expected. Emily did present an opportunity to replant endemic trees, very few of which were damaged. Many parts of the Island were without electricity for up to three weeks and though we weathered the hurricane remarkably well, the unsightly power lines were hard hit. It has been suggested that these lines should be laid underground, an expensive but worthwhile undertaking from both a practical and aesthetic point of view. In the background is Darrell's Island which has a varied history.

Named for the Darrell family, it carries the old form of the name - Dorrel - on the early Norwood maps and was later used as a quarantine centre for smallpox and yellow fever victims and passengers and crew who had come from yellow fever ports. During the 19th Century, Bermuda suffered through at least nine epidemics of yellow fever, also known as "yellow flag" in reference to the colour of the quarantine flag that a ship had to fly if there were contagious diseases on board. The earliest of these epidemics occurred in 1699 and once started, the disease spread quickly, killing many people, especially newcomers, within days. Various types of cures were attempted though the cause was only discovered earlier this century. Many of the marshes and ponds became landfill projects to reduce mosquito breeding grounds.

In June, 1901, the island was used as an encampment for 1,100 Boer prisoners of war, with its own church, library, school, dining and wash tents and authority to run their own affairs. Prisoners were also held on five other islands in the Great Sound.

In the 1930s, the island became Bermuda's marine airport. In 1937 a million-dollar terminal building was erected on the island, and Bermuda became a mid-Atlantic sea-plane airport. During World War II, it grew in importance as the "clippers" made their way back and forth across the Atlantic. With the construction of the airport in St. David's, civilian land aircraft were introduced and Darrell's Island was closed. It would lie derelict until 1954, when a company was formed with combined Bermudian and American money to produce television films. Despite an enthuisiastic start, the venture soon ran out of money and was closed within four months. The island is now owned by the Government and is used as a summer camp site.

This tree is at Belmont Manor. The original house was built by Mr. John Wainright in 1815 and was incorporated into the present hotel. The house had high ceilings and large doors because Mr. Wainwright suffered from rheumatism so his horse was brought to his bedroom and he mounted it from his bed.

FAIRY LIGHTS
Harbour Road, Warwick

Warwick is named for Lord Robert Rich, 2nd Earl of Warwick, whose father, like the Earl of Devonshire, donated roughly 10,000 pounds to King James for a hunting expedition, so securing his earldom. The Earl's mother, Penelope, was the sister of the ill-fated Earl of Essex who divorced Warwick and married the Earl of Devonshire. In 1616 the 2nd Earl was told about Bermuda by a cousin of the same name and subsequently bought the maximum of 15 shares from Sir Robert Mansell. He then sent cattle out to his tenants and had them grow tobacco, sugar-cane and grapes. The Company decided to change the name of Mansell's Tribe to that of Warwick.

Harbour Road is named for obvious reasons and is the most scenic of Bermuda's main arteries. The road is very narrow, however, with few straight sections.

PASS OVER
Khyber Pass, Warwick

Warwick Pond, in the background of the photograph, is one of several sinkholes which range along the main body of Bermuda. Originally caves formed in the Ice Age, they became basins when their roofs collapsed under the weight of heavy rainfall. The basins could well have started life as beaches set between lines of hills which were originally great sand dunes left stranded when the water level lowered at the end of the Ice Age, leaving harbours, coves, marshes and ponds.

Warwick Pond is now frequented by wild birds migrating south in the winter. One of the few havens for birds at the western end of the Island, it has been preserved in perpetuity thanks to Mr. Dennis Sherwin, a former president of the Bermuda National Trust, who bought the property for the Trust.

At the western end of the Pond, you can see the unusual spire of St. Mary's, the parish church for Warwick. The present church was built in 1832, replacing the original which was one of the first four built in Bermuda in the early 1600s. Diarist Harriet Suzette Lloyd tells of a funeral she attended there: "The pallbearers on this occasion were ladies, wives of the principal inhabitants...The solemnity of the service, the wild flickering of the lights, which just served to make the darkness visible and shed a faint gleam on the altar, the foreign countenances of the negroes, the loud sob of the female relatives all combined to make an impression I shall never forget."

Khyber Pass begins opposite the church and is one of the deepest stone cuts on the Island. In the foreground of the photograph is an example of a more recent quarry. Almost all of Bermuda's earliest homes are built from Bermuda stone which was quarried in this way and the stone was also used for ships' ballast. The stone is still used today, primarily for roof slate.

SAFE PASSAGE
Point Shares, Pembroke

Point Shares is one of the oldest place names in Bermuda and it was owned for 200 years by the Stowes, an important early family. It was later bought by General Russell Hastings, a veteran of the American Civil War, who retired to Bermuda in 1880 because the local climate was kinder to the injuries he received in the fighting than the colder American weather.

General Hastings became a British subject, built Soncy, whose Bay is shown in Halcyon Days, and settled into Bermuda life with his family. General Hastings is remembered as one of the founders of the Bermuda High School for girls, and also for having put the Easter Lily bulb industry on a commercial basis.

Point Shares Road passes Soncy and crosses a narrow causeway separating Fairyland water from a palm fringed pool and then diverges into a spiders web of drives leading to some of the most exlusive homes on the Island.

WARWICK LONG BAY

Warwick Long Bay begins a stretch of the Island's most beautiful South Shore beaches, including Christian, Horseshoe and Stonehole bays which are pictured below. As William Zuill said in Bermuda Journey: "...One must discover the delights of the South Shore for himself. An inadequate attempt to describe the allure of a region at once so diversified, so lovely and so untouched by development, will not greatly tempt the explorer, while any remarks he makes for himself will render the remarks superfluous."

CHRISTMAS DAY 1990
Stonehole Bay, Warwick

No prizes for guessing why it's called Stonehole Bay. Bermuda is generally very lucky with the weather and over the two-day celebration either Christmas or Boxing Day is usually sunny. 1990 was gorgeous with little wind, eighty degree heat and the South Shore swell accentuating it all. Bermudians call their Island "God's Country" and refer to their parish specifically as such, sparking some very good humoured dialogue when the reference occurs.

PUT OUT TO PASTURE
Watch Hill, Warwick

This rustic scene has nostalgia written all over it. Unfortunately Esso the Lamb has died, Bessy the Bike has further deteriorated but Bert the Bathtub is still enjoying his perch under Cedric the Cedar.

Watch Hill is a charming old farmstead that still hosts an animal house thanks to Anne Powell, whose amazing energy enables friends and children to enjoy Bermuda's dying rural heritage. Originally named Rose Hill, the property was first sold for five shillings and a peppercorn.

The quaint cottage on Middle Road, at the bottom of the property, was the home of the Warwick Watch policeman. The cottage also served as a butcher's shop and a "house of ill repute" - the madame charged two shillings and sixpence for her favours, primarily to servicemen.

HORSEPOWER
Horseshoe Bay, Southampton

Since Hurricane Emily caught the Island off guard, much more care, respect and attention has been paid to storms and hurricanes. The Island has not been hit as hard since Emily but as this shot of Hurricane Lily shows we do live on a fragile and precarious rock. Hurricane Lily sideswiped the island and did no real damage (a little erosion on the South Shore) so we all wait for the next direct hit.

JEKYLL AND HYDE
Horseshoe Bay, Southampton

Taken from the same angle on Christmas Day 1990, this shows the contrast of winter light and weather conditions. Mild winters are an attraction to North Americans who come for cultural enlightenment provided by the Bermuda Festival and the Island's museums and the odd day like this. There is so much to see and visit that mild temperatures benefit these activities in winter rather than during the hot and humid summer. A more realistic flavour of the Island is gleaned when there is less activity and traffic.

This little bay is the western end of the South Shore Park which also hosts Warwick Camp where for three years young draftees must endure military regimens. The effectiveness of military training for the defence of the island has been called into question on occasion. Forced servitude for military purposes does tend to breed resentment towards authority, especially when draft selection seems random. A combination of community service with basic military training undertaken by all of Bermuda's youth might be a more fair and effective approach.

SPANISH POINT

Prior to settlement, Spanish Point was probably an early encampment for shipwrecked mariners who would live off the plentiful fish, wild hogs and birds which populated the isle. Explorers from the Sea Venture found the remains of an encampment and other signs that indicated a recent visit from Spaniards - so they called the place Spanish Point. This was substantiated in this century when Spanish archives revealed the visit of a Captain Ramirez in 1603.

According to the records, Ramirez' ship was driven, intact, into the Great Sound during a storm. He sent ashore a landing party to find water as night fell. The birds on shore started to chatter and the Spaniards thought these were the devils which gave Bermuda one of its early names, the Isles of Devils. The water party came back to the boat, exclaiming, "What devils are these? The boat's rudder is broken!" Ramirez sent a negro, Venturilla, ashore with a lantern to cut a piece of wood to replace the rudder. Venturilla landed and disappeared into the bushes where he began to yell. Ramirez shouted: "The devil is carrying off the negro! All ashore!" When the crew landed they were assaulted by unseen enemies which they soon realised were not devils but birds, and they killed 500 of them. They would live off birds for the remainder of their stay.

Ramirez drew up a map of the Island and also set up large crosses with directions on them in Spanish telling future visitors where to find water. This cross was later mistaken by English settlers as an indication of buried treasure.

Spanish Point marks the western end of Pembroke and is also notable for the strange wreck which can be seen in the two photographs at left. In 1869, the largest floating dock of the time was dispatched from England for the Dockyard - the first time a dock had been towed aross the ocean. Her safe arrival was regarded as a triumph for the Royal Navy and she was greeted by huge crowds on land and at sea.

"The whole town of Hamilton seemed to have come to stare at this strange monster - the most wonderful craft that ever made voyage since Noah's Ark went cruising," an officer wrote. By 1904 the old dock had been superseded by a new, larger dock, the "Bermuda", and was condemned. The hull was sold to an American firm of ship breakers, but as she was towed away, her cables parted and the craft was driven into the bay at Spanish Point, where she remains to this day.

The central picture shows the short distance between Spanish Point and Dockyard. Until the 19th Century, it was impossible for large vessels to enter the Great Sound and to use Hamilton Harbour. Under Admiral Dundonald, a channel was dredged between the reefs which guarded the Sound, enabling larger warships and merchant vessels to enter the Great Sound. Not only did the dredging of the channel - and the creation later of Two Rock Passage - help the establishment of the Dockyard, but it would lay some of the groundwork for the Island's cruise ship and tourism industry. The island at centre is Tilly Island.

Beek Rock provides a great point of view for those who don't mind getting their feet wet (second from right). The Beakes were a respected 17th Century family and in 1646 Richard Beake, described as "an aged schoolmaster" wrote a long letter of protest that he had endured 13 months' imprisonment owing to implacable religious dissensions and spiritual tyranny. On this note, Jane Hopkins, one of the passengers on the Mayflower in 1620, "reached Bermuda only to be indicted and executed as a witch 1655". (Bermudiana)

Pembroke was called Spanish Point and was obviously somewhat backward as this verse tells us:
All the way to Spanish Point,
There the times are out of joint.

'ROUND THE ISLAND SEAGULL RACE
Long Island, The Great Sound

One of Bermuda's most colourful days and certainly one of the most ridiculous. In about 1970 a friendly challenge transpired between two fishermen to see who could reach their fishing grounds first. One of the two raced with a seagull engine while the other had a much larger outboard. This humourous encounter evolved into a most profound challenge. An invitation was extended to all craft in Devonshire Bay to race around the Island powered solely by British Seagull outboard engines. A product of Victorian engineering, the Seagull engine has "the" reputation for reliability and ranges in horsepower from a mighty 1.5 to a menacing 6.

   The inaugural race saw the participation of about 10 vessels of varying descriptions, each with a crew of two. Participation increased to a peak of 55 to 60 craft but sadly the race went into recession (1987 saw only four competitors). Fortunately for civilization and contrary to world trends the race has since boomed - 25 dinghies raced in 1990. This epic circumcolonial expedition still adheres to the original rules of play - around the Island without passing under any bridges, a Seagull engine, a case of beer (due to the advent of "light weight" planing dinghies) and standard safety equipment. The record for the Devonshire Bay race was a blistering three hours and fifty-nine minutes. The current course commences from the "Eye of the Needle" at the west end of Long Island, increasing the already painful distance from 32 to 36 nautical miles. The last craft to cross the finish line in 1990 took a gruelling ten hours.

   The colourful tradition of "the Race" has been enthusiastically nurtured and preserved. The respective crews deport themselves in widely ranging styles, from the very casual to the utterly bizarre. The boat names describe eloquently the hilarity of the occasion - Hasty Puddin', Wharf Rat, Fuzzy Duck, Roaring Snail, The $90 Experiment, Screaming Flea, Happy Snapper, Rigid Mortus, Cookin' With Gaas, Terrapin Flyer, Strictly Bubblin' and more. As time goes on the boats are becoming more outrageous in design and finish. Roguery abounds .

   Underlying the frivolity is a serious undercurrent of rivalry. There are presently three racing classes:
"A", cruising and traditional dinghies. The 1991 season will see the advent of "the serious seablade"- a multi-engine.

   The British Seagull company has released a new "racing" engine which has injected life into the race for those who are seriously vying for "the record" .

   Keep it up.

SPLENDID ISOLATION
Gamma Island, The Great Sound

Gamma Island is one of many islands scattered throughout the Great Sound named after the Greek alphabet and is now a summer residence.

MUSCLE IN
Riddells Bay, Southampton

This serene view was captured in the late summer while going out for a sunset cruise. We chanced upon this fella hunting for something at low tide. In the background is the amalgamation of "The Brothers", Tucker Island and Morgan's Island, now the United

States Naval Annex, part of the "lend-lease" agreement. Colonel Henry Tucker (the Gunpowder Plot), bought Tucker Island in 1759 from James Rivers, thus eventually changing the name of the island from Rivers to Tucker. During the Boer War this island housed 800 prisoners, most of whom had sworn the Oath of Allegiance to Great Britain and had to be separated from the other prisoners for their own safety.

Morgan's Island was named for a Captain Morgan who assisted Henry Tucker in the Gunpowder Plot. Morgan's Cloud, which occurs during the summer when a long line of cloud hangs over the island, is named for Capt. Morgan. An old man on the day of the Gunpowder Plot was heard to say that the deed would be "a dark cloud hanging over Bermuda".

With the end of the Cold War and impending defence cuts, the Annex will be returned to Bermuda in 1993, before the end of their 99-year lease. However, the Americans have regrettably stopped their maintenance programme of the buildings. These buildings include some old houses (one is 115 years old) that have intrinsic value to Bermuda because they are the only reminder of "the Brothers" past history. Old Bermuda houses require constant maintenance to prevent them from deteriorating. To hand back the Annex and its Bermudian buildings in disrepair would be a sad ending to their long tenancy.

WATER LOGGED
Jews Bay, Southampton

This picture is taken from the Waterlot Inn in Southampton and shows Jews Bay which was probably named to counter Christian Bay on the South Shore. The Waterlot has been a well-known restaurant and inn for most of this century and was painstakingly restored after a fire in the 1970s.

CHILD'S PLAY
Christian Bay, Southampton

This is the beach of "The Reefs", one of several small Bermudian-owned hotels and cottage colonies with excellent reputations for good service and high levels of ,repeat visitors. Some people are so in love with Bermuda that they return year after year.

Southampton Parish gets its name from Henry, the 3rd Earl of Southampton, who was involved in the conspiracy, mentioned earlier, of the Earl of Essex. The young earl's sentence of execution was commuted to life imprisonment upon the intervention of influential supporters. He, like Sir Thomas Smith, was released by King James. The Hampton River in the US is also named for Henry who had a great interest in the colonisation of North America.

"GIBRALTAR OF THE WEST"
Dockyard, Ireland Island
Sandys

Bermuda's role as the "Gibraltar of the West" began after Britain lost the American Revolutionary War and her bases on the American eastern seaboard. The emergence of the United States as a military power meant Britain had to establish secure bases in the Atlantic which could fend off the young country's threat to British marine interests. Bermuda was at first ruled out as a base because the Navy did not believe it provided safe anchorages for her ships and the reefs surrounding the Island were thought to be impenetrable for large ships of the line. In the 1790s, a survey by the Navy established Murray's Anchorage as a safe, deep-water harbour and Bermuda's connection with the Royal Navy, which continues to this day, began.

Land around the island was purchased and work on Dockyard, the most visible symbol of Britain's military might in 19th Century Bermuda, began in 1809. Much of the early work was carried out by convicts, but some Bermudians were also involved in its construction. One, John Lee, was still employed in 1930, having been born 100 years earlier. His father had worked there before him, and he could still remember the days of the convicts and the hulks they were forced to inhabit. His longevity was not hurt by his consumption of "quantities of the raw and potent black rum which has driven the white man to suicide and worse", according to *Bermuda Journey*. The convicts were used for 40 years, until 1863 when penal labour was abolished. The convicts' tenure took a terrible toll. Some 2,000 out of the 9,000 who served on the hulks died of disease during this time. Often the crimes which drew transportation sentences were minor. One Bermuda convict was sentenced to two years on the hulks for stealing his father's horse!

In 1951, the Royal Navy stopped repairing ships in Bermuda and began to reduce its presence. Today there is just a small base at HMS Malabar on Ireland Island, and there has been talk of combining its operations there with the US Navy who would give up the Annex.

When the Navy closed Dockyard and the British Army withdrew its garrisons at Prospect and St. George's, the Bermuda Government bought the land and planned to use Dockyard as a free port area for light industry. The scheme had only limited success and for some 20 years the Dockyard went into gentle decline, uncared for and rarely visited. This ended in the early 1970s when a group of Bermudians interested in Bermuda's long romance with the sea, saw the potential of using the Keepyard as a maritime museum. The main exhbition hall was opened in 1975 by Queen Elizabeth II and the museum has since been developed further and is a popular tourist attraction.

The rest of the Dockyard is now being redeveloped by a Government subsidised company which has installed a cruise ship dock and areas for shops, restaurants and a small movie theatre. These developments may make the area as busy as it was when it was run by the Royal Navy.

The Clocktower building in the foreground of this picture has been developed as a shopping arcade but once housed workshops..While one of the towers does indeed feature a clock, the other is a tide gauge. The building on the left hand side of the photograph is Casemates, Bermuda's only high security prison. It is now being replaced with a new complex to its west. Before becoming a jail, it was a Royal Navy barracks for many years.

BARKEEP
Commissioner's Point, Sandys

Commissioner's House in the Keepyard is a classic example of a civil servant who had ideas above his station. It was begun in 1824 by a Commissioner of the Dockyard who wanted a home which would live up to his exaggerated idea of his own importance. Four years later, 400,000 pounds had been spent on the building - a huge sum in those days - and the building was not yet completed. A contemporary account said: "Gradually a palace arose, such as few Governors in the largest colonies (except India) have ever possessed."

It was decorated with mahogany woodwork, marble fireplaces and Yorkshire stone for the verandahs. It also had a marble bath with piped salt, fresh and hot water and stables for 11 horses and two carriages, although Ireland Island was one mile long and accessible only by boat.

The Commissioner never lived in his mansion as he went mad before it was completed and his successors only used it for 10 years. It was later used as a barracks and is now being carefully restored by the Maritime Museum.

Sandys Parish is named for Sir Edwin Sandys who greeted King James on the Scottish-English border in 1605 and was knighted on the spot. He was, after Sir Francis Bacon, the most respected Parliamentarian of his day.

POT SHOT
Jew's Bay, Southampton

In July 1988 an environmental pressure group made up of young Bermudians, Friends of Fish, was formed to create more public awareness of problems with the reefs and declining fish stocks. Its objective was to have legislation enacted to ban pot fishing, an indiscriminate method of entrapping reef fish. On January 28th 1990, the Minister of the Environment announced a complete ban with compensation for the fishermen. The move was controversial as more than 70 fishermen and their crews had to change their livelihoods, but the majority of the community welcomed it as a sensible act of environmental protection. The fishpot ban was inevitable but was hastened by the *group and other public pressure. In enacting the ban, the Government agreed to a Commission of Inquiry to examine the fishing industry and the marine environment. In February 1991 the Commission made recommendations that would protect Bermuda's waters which were sensible and far reaching and biased towards neither side. If implemented, our future will be much more promising as this final Friends of Fish advertisement succinctly reveals:*

HATS OFF TO THE MINISTER OF THE ENVIRONMENT AND ALL THOSE WHO APPRECIATE MARINE LIFE AROUND THIS ISLAND
THE FIRST AND MOST DIFFICULT STEP HAS BEEN TAKEN

The reef fish keep the reef clean. The reefs break the seas up and thus our beaches and shorelines are protected. If the reefs deteriorate the beaches will be washed away and our shoreline will erode.

NO REEF FISH=EROSION OF REEF=EROSION OF BERMUDA

Approximately one third of our populations' employment relies on the tourist industry. Our marine environment is one of the most valuable attractions, therefore it is vital to preserve tourist related jobs. In short, it's obviously better for the Unions and all of Bermuda to support the majority who need to be employed versus a limited number (71) who unintentionally are killing their own livelihoods.

NO REEF FISH=NO TOURISM=NO JOBS=NO FUTURE

All parties and independents in the last election promised to enact legislation to protect our reefs. Now they are doing it as has been done in the past.

1620 - An act against the killing of young tortoises
1791 - An act to prohibit the setting of fish pots
1891 - The Fish Net Act
1990 - Ban on fish pots

This is for the good of all Bermudians. This must be done so that our fish stocks can replenish and all our children and grandchildren will have an island to stand on and reef fish to enjoy.
EXTINCTION IS FOREVER..!
FRIENDS OF FISH

GREAT SOUND EFFECT
The Great Sound, Southampton

The environment needs continual monitoring and legislation to ensure its protection and to avoid controversies like the fish pot ban. While the Government has tried to manage our environment there are areas which have been overlooked. There is a growing appreciation that the problem of waste management needs to be addressed, as many of our inshore waters are showing the effects of seepage from cesspits and barely-treated sewage being pumped into the ocean. The island has had several droughts in recent years and a full programme of sewage treatment would help our water supplies. Not only would this end contamination of the Island's fresh water lenses and inshore waters but treated sewage can be used to irrigate parks, golf courses, gardens and be recycled as flushing water. The Greenhouse Effect is upon us and the Island has the opportunity to demonstrate that by producing a Great Sound Effect we can have our own Greenhouse Effect.

Equally, Bermuda still has to come to grips with the problems of waste management and the "throwaway society". With landfills overflowing, Government is in the process of building an incinerator - which may need additional safety devices - and has taken the first tentative steps towards recycling. But solving the problem of managing waste has to be supported by the whole community and this will only come with greater awareness and the application of the "three Rs" - Reduce, Re-use, Recycle.

SWEPT CLEAN
Seaswept Farm, Southampton

Seaswept Farm is a property of some 26 acres and this field has just been turned over to bananas. Bermuda bananas are smaller and sweeter than other commercial varieties.

FLOATSTONES
Mangrove Bay, Sandys

King's Point in Mangrove Bay is at the very end of Somerset Island. Sandys Parish is most often referred to as Somerset, originally "Somers Seate". While the Sea Venture castaways were in Bermuda, Sir George Somers explored and charted the island and became so fond of Somerset Island that it was named for him.

Mangrove Bay was obviously named for the trees that once lined its shores and in the late 18th and early 19th centuries the Parish was also known as Mangrove Bay. The verse of that time for the westernmost parish runs:

All the way to Mangrove Bay,
There the old maids go to stay.

DANGLING CARROTS
Near Overplus Lane, Sandys

Very near this alluring field is the site of the earliest land dispute in Bermuda. When Governor Daniel Tucker arrived in Bermuda in 1616, his main objective was to see that the Island was divided into tribes and shares. Norwood's survey left a surplus of 200 acres on the Southampton-Sandys border that was said to be very good, protected farmland. Tucker set about building a house on the land which was called Overplus. Many of the colonists objected to this behaviour and complained to the Company in London which took action but only succeeded in recouping some of the land as possession was nine tenths of the law.

MAKIN' TRACKS
Bushy Park, Sandys

This is what old Bermuda was like. It is wonderful to see that its old world character is still valued. Seen at left is one of the most amazing stands of cedar trees in Bermuda. They have required great love and attention to reach this stage having been planted 11 years ago.

SPRING FIELD
Somerset Island, Sandys

In the 19th Century, farmers grew spring vegetables for the rapidly growing northern cities of the United States. Onions and potatoes were among the earliest exports, the former giving Bermudians their nickname of "Onions". Refrigeration and improved transport in the United States contributed to the decline of the industry and Bermuda's small farmers were never able to compete with their big American competitors. In the late 1920s some farmers in the southern US states named their hometowns Bermuda and thus were able to sell "Bermuda onions". At the same time protectionism in the US was growing, and import duties were steadily increased. The final blow came in 1930 with the passage of the Smoot-Hawley Act in the US, which made Bermuda produce completely uncompetitive in the US. Exports were returned to Bermuda where they rotted on the docks. Today, tourism is the main industry and very little is exported except a few lilies.

The retention of the few remaining farms on the Island is essential, and many are now zoned as arable land. Not only do they reinforce Bermudians' links with the land, but these open spaces, as much as any park, serve as "green lungs" where residents and visitors can "breathe" away from the rest of the island's suburban sprawl.

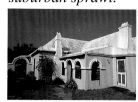

SPRINGFIELD
Somerset Island, Sandys

This is another of the National Trust's properties. Alongside the house is the Gilbert Nature Reserve which can be seen in Spring Field on the left of the field. Springfield was the home of the Gilbert family and was in their possession for nine generations. The rambling buildings now house the Somerset library and Government's Springfield Nursery School. The buttery roof of this complex is referred to earlier in the book under "Tucked In".

WANTED DEAD AND ALIVE
St. James' Church, Sandys

This beautifully proportioned church's spire was designed by Dr. Henry Hinson who was an amateur architect. He also designed the spires for St. Mark's, Smith's; St. Paul's, Paget; St. Paul's A.M.E., Hamilton. St. James was rebuilt in 1789 after the hurricane of 1780 destroyed the original church. A thunderbolt hit the spire earlier this century and caused some damage to the eastern end. It must be one of the only churches in the world to face west. The entrance to the church was from Daniel's Head Road but when Church Hill Road was built, the arrangement was reversed.

The cedar tree seen here demonstrates a strange phenomena that has occurred in the past two decades. Some cedar trees regenerate themselves and eventually the live part will take over the whole tree. Bermuda has a long tradition of religious tolerance with many denominations and more churches per square mile than anywhere else in the world. With virtual self-government the practicalities of life were encouraged rather than religious adherence, although fines were imposed on those who chose to work on the Seventh day.

WHALE WATCHING
West Whale Bay, Southampton

There were six important whaling stations in Bermuda at one time, with three in St. David's and the remaining three at Whale Bay, Paget Island and Tucker's Town. Thankfully the whaling industry is now purely a spectator sport in Bermuda. There has been a small increase in these majestic creatures in the past few years and many Bermudians watch as they pass close to the Island on their migration each spring providing a unique opportunity for close observation by whale watchers and scientists, and an unadvertised tourist attraction. The old colloquial name for Southampton was Port Royal, and a nearby golf course retains the name. Whale Bay Fort, above the beach, also overlooks the course.

BACK TO THE DRAWING BOARD
Somerset Bridge, Sandys

Somerset Bridge has the distinction of being the smallest drawbridge in the world. The drawbridge is just a single plank which allows the masts of small sailboats to be guided through by hand. The bridge is almost never used for this purpose now because of dramatic increases in traffic and a corresponding decline in recreational use of small sailboats.

The bridge was proposed in 1620 in the effort to link the 700 acre island to the Main, making access throughout the Island easier. This is also the site of some interesting social history as Bermuda Journey relates:"During the eighteenth century a strong communtiy life developed among the families at Somerset Bridge, and in 1765 these excellent folk formed a remarkable club which endured for upwards of seventy years. This was called the Somerset Bridge Club, and among its objectives was the acquisition of a library containing 'all the books on economics in whatever language they have been written'. Unemployment was seen to be a danger, and members pledged themselves to find work 'suitable to their character for all lawful persons of both sexes', while a reward was offered to everyone who introduced into the colony 'any new art or improvement to one already known'. Finally this extraordinary society dealt with the old-age pensions - a question which we are apt to think has only been recognised in our modern, state-aided civilization; the club proposed to pension 'all day labourers of unblemished reputation who after forty years of assiduous labour had not been able to amass a sufficient sum to make their latter days glide onward to their goal without inquietude'.

"As we contemplate these lofty aspirations from the distance of our own disillusioned era, let us listen to an observer of a century ago who, likewise impressed with the Somerset Bridge Club, remarked that their purposes were 'perhaps the most respectable monument which has ever honored humanity'."

ELYSIAN FIELDS
Ely's Harbour, Sandys

Ely's Harbour is named for William Eli who arrived and settled in Bermuda in 1621, though little else is known of the man. The harbour was the centre for boat building in the Somerset area and many sleek vessels were turned out of her yards. Bethell's Island, Palm Island and Morgan Island provide excellent protection of the harbour throughout the year. These three islands have an appropriate nickname - The Movie Set. In the background on the right is Daniel's Island named after Governor Daniel Tucker. Just to the left of the island is Chubb Cut Channel which was the only approach to the island through the reefs in the West End.

The harbour was also the site of a bizarre tale of an abandoned ship, as Ronald Williams' *Bermudiana* tells: "Of the hundreds of strange tales told of wrecked ships in Bermuda waters, perhaps the most improbable is that of the MINERVA, Bermuda built and Bermudian owned, which in 1849 sailed out of Ely's in Sandy's Parish. She was a stoutly-built cedar vessel and was bound for Africa and the Far East. From evidence later available it appears that when far out in the Atlantic or perhaps in the Indian Ocean she encountered a gale which rendered her unseaworthy in the opinion of her captain. In any event she was abandoned at sea, and no member of the ship's company was seen again. But, more than 2 years after the Minerva left her home port, residents on the shores of Ely's harbour awoke one morning to see a familiar looking vessel lying on her side in the virtually land-locked reaches of the bay. The ship was a derelict and was indentified as the Minerva. No man, alive or dead, was on board, but in the cabin was found the ship's log book. The last entry in the log had been made 14 months earlier, indicating that the abandoned ship had drifted with ocean currents for more than a year, finally to come to rest, incredibly, in the very harbour from which she had set out 2 years before."

More recently another mystery ocurred on Bethell's Island when a headless skeleton was uncovered during renovations. There is no recorded history to explain this occurrence but with carbon dating methods the time period at least may be established. Ely's Harbour is the location of the notorious murder of Anna Skeeters in 1878 by her husband Edward, who threw Anna's body into the ocean weighted by a boulder. This boulder became Skeeters' grave headstone on Burt's Island after his execution.

HERON'S HAUNT
Wreck Hill, Sandys

Wreck Hill was named after a Flemish wreck which appears on Sir George Somers' map. The hill was also one of the earliest settlements on the Island and the site of an early fort.

In 1775, the Bermudians who stole gunpowder from the magazine in St. George's for the American revolutionaries came ashore here and rolled the 10 cannons at the fort into the sea. It is said that all but one of the guns remain there to this day. The date for this incident is also said to be1777 - unrelated to the Plot.

Wreck House is now owned by Australian impresario Robert Stigwood, who has painstakingly restored the old home and the surrounding buildings.

The most westerly point in Bermuda, Wreck Hill was where the inhabitants searched the horizon for shipwrecks. At one time, the hill was covered in great cedar trees, but these were lost in the blight. Mr. Stigwood has planted more than 1,000 trees on the property, an example other landowners, including the Government, would do well to follow.

Herons are frequently seen in Ely's Harbour as it is relatively peaceful and lined with mangroves at harbour's southern limit. These waders are timid and do not like to be approached.

DEAD SET ON
Palm Island, Sandys

This keystone of The Movie Set and Morgan Island to the west are owned by the National Trust. The dead cedar trees provide Bermuda with an unusual landscape of sculptures, each with their own character. There is a strain of cedar tree that grows straight up, much like the Norfolk Pine and these were the trees preferred for shipbuilding.

A FITTING START
Mangrove Bay, Sandys

Few pictures can demonstrate Bermuda's long and unusual marine history as the start of a Bermuda Fitted Dinghy race.. The dinghies are pulled along the side of the start boat, a unique way to start a sailing race. The boats are handicapped to make the races more exciting and are closely followed by locals who cheer on their favourite boat. These racing vessels are unique in that they are 14 feet 1 inch long and carry 1,000 sqare feet of sail downwind. When Uffa Fox, an English sailing legend, heard of our dinghies he did not believe that they would even float. The dinghies have three sets of sails and are "fitted" appropriately for our varied wind conditions. Misjudgement on the fit leads to sinking. Fitted Dinghies require great skill to sail. When competitive sail racing started in Bermuda, vessels of varying size (handicapped by one minute per foot of keel length) were manned by mainly black professional crews competing against each other of large purses.

The dinghies provide the link to the early days of Bermuda sailing when the 'Bermuda rig' was pioneered. Mentioned previously, Bermudians fine-tuned the most effective windward rig, adapting the Jamaica 'rig' of the early 1600s. As a small, isolated country trading salt initially, the best defense against attack on the high seas was effective evasion! It has now become the most common method of fitting small boats and racing yachts but before the days of steam, Bermuda-built boats traded all over the world and were used by the Royal Navy as fast sloops. These fast and durable craft were commissioned by the Americans, privateers and traders. Their reputation for speed was unsurpassed and in 1805, a Bermuda-built sloop, the Pickle, carried the news of Nelson's victory and death at Trafalgar back to England.

HAPPY SNAPPING
The Happy Snapper is one of the last dinghies built by Mr. Geary Pitcher, who is the last traditional boat-builder on the Island. Born in 1904, Mr. Pitcher is still building his "dinkies" as we go to press. It will be a very sad day for Bermuda when these seaworthy boats are no longer made.

THE NORTHERN REEFS

North of Bermuda, the reefs continue for a few miles and there are many known shipwrecks here. In 1593, Henry May became the first Englishman to set foot on Bermuda. He was returning to England aboard a French boat, the "Bonaventure", when it ran aground on North Rock, a forty foot rock on the north-west outer reef. The ship's crew salvaged their tools from the wreck and spent the next few months on the Island building another ship.

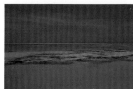

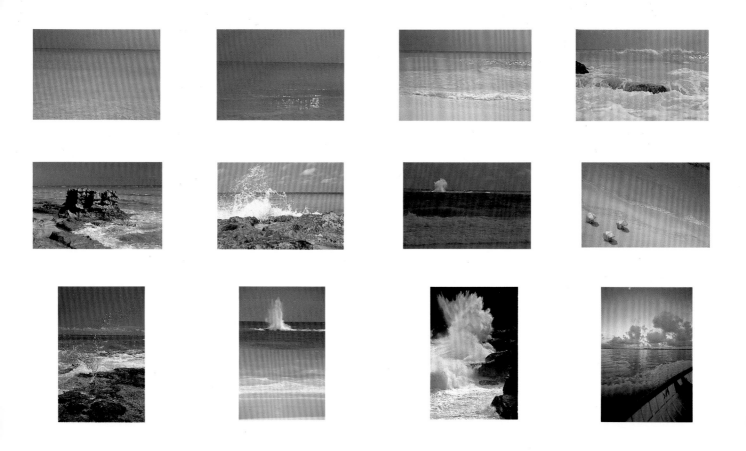

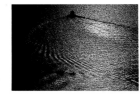
Bermuda's waters are magnificent and ever changing. Though many words and pictures may try to describe and do justice, the feelings experienced when near the ocean are always intensely personal. The Island is spared from ocean swells by the protective reefs, providing Bermuda's people with an enviable natural resource. The surrounding water is very turbulent due to the warm Gulf Stream meeting with cold Northern currents and Sir Walter Raleigh said in 1595 that Bermuda's water was "a hellish sea for thunder, lightning and storms". Had Sir Walter ventured further into our little oasis, he would have found a different situation.

Thanks to the Naval Oceanography Command Facility for their help identifying the various cloud formations in these cloudscapes.

PUFF THE MAGIC CLOUD

Cirrus and cirrostratus surround Puff which is a cumulonimbus "low 2" cloud in its formative stages. At the top left is Stratocumulus.

THE ALTO PEACE

This interesting scape contains Alto and Stratocumulus with Cirrus in the background.

FEATHER IN THE CAP

This is a mature Cumulonimbus formation with additional battlements being formed to the right of the main cell. A Cumulus tower is being formed at the back.

CUMULATIVE EFFECT

This is Altocumulus with Cumulonimbus and Towering Cumulus on the horizon.

TWO-BIT CLOUD

A very early morning shot captured this Cumulonimbus.

MOUSETRAP

Part of the same cloud formation as Two-Bit Cloud, this is Cirrus spreading out with very turbulent winds aloft. Battlements forming are being blown back by the wind, referred to as shearing.

SHEARWATER

"Shearwater" was running from the rain shower falling from this Cumulus cloud.

NUCLEAR RAIN

This is Puff the Magic Cloud about 30 minutes later after it had developed into a mature Cumulonimbus formation. Cirrus surrounds the cloud.

WHISPERING PALMS

Here is a classic example of Cirrostratus fibratus or Cs.

KEEPING UP WITH

In this shot Stratocumulus is in the foreground while the remaining cloud is Altocumulus.

TAKIN' LICKS

This magnificent sky consists of two super-imposed layers of Altocumulus with the upper being Translucidus and the lower being Translucidus perlucidus.

AND SOME HAVE ONE OF GOLD

Gold outlines this Towering Cumulus. There is also Cumulus Congestus present.

LUNATIC FRINGES

This October full moon is accentuated by Cirrostratus.

RAISE HELL

Part of the same sunset/moonrise this is also Cirrostratus with the lower layer on the horizon being Stratocumulus.

SNAKE CHARMER

This slippery formation of Altostratus is nestled between a lower and upper layer of Stratocumulus.

LOOK WHO FRAMED CHARLIE AND THE PINK RABBIT!

The rabbit is Cumulus Congestus while its ears are Cirrus.

DREAMSCAPE

Altocumulus floats in the middle of this scape while Stratocumulus rides below. There is also high Cirrus but this is not predominant.

IN DUST REAL

The industrial clouds floating about are Stratocumulus with lighter industrial Cirrostratus streaks. The bright line at left is Altostatus.

MEAN SEA LEVEL

This type of tropical wave is common for Bermuda and the formation is not convective, merely an unstable atmospheric wave that moves from east to west.

RAISE IN HEAVEN

This cloud formation has Stratocumulus written all over it.

SPECTRACULAR

This mystical and natural phenomena is called a sun glint, which highlights a low layer of Stratocumulus with a high layer of Cirrus and Cirrostratus.

A SCAPE

The lower cloud here is Stratocumulus with Cumulus peaking above. The streaks are AltoCumulus.

B.C.

B.C. looks like Bermuda abstracted and also resembles a foetus. For any Bermudian wondering where "God's Country" really is , here is the answer, the East End where most of Bermuda's roots really are! I do expect some disagreement but this picture is hard to argue with.

138

BIBLIOGRAPHY

Arnell, J.C. - Sailing in Bermuda. Royal Hamilton Amateur Dinghy Club, Bermuda 1982
Benbow, Colin. - Boer Prisoners of War in Bermuda Second edition. The Bermuda College 1982
Tucker, Terry. - The Islands of Bermuda. Bermuda 1970 (updated 1979)
Wilkinson, Henry. - Bermuda From Sail to Steam Vols I and II. Oxford University Press, London 1973
Wilkinson, Henry. - The Adventurers of Bermuda Second Edition. Oxford University Press, London 1958
Williams, Ronald. - Bermudiana. The Bermudian Publishing Company 1936
Zuill, William E.S. - Bermuda Journey. The Bermuda Book Stores, 1946
Zuill, William S. - The Story of Bermuda and Her People. MacMillan, London 1972